THE
PRESS BOOK

THE PRESS BOOK

ADVENTURES AND MISADVENTURES IN PRINT MEDIA

Brian Braithwaite

Peter Owen
London and Chester Springs, PA, USA

PETER OWEN PUBLISHERS
73 Kenway Road, London SW5 0RE

Peter Owen books are distributed in the USA by
Dufour Editions Inc., Chester Springs, PA 19425-0007

First published in Great Britain 2009 by Peter Owen Publishers
© Brian Braithwaite 2009

ISBN 978-0-7206-1333-9

A catalogue record for this book is available from
the British Library.

Printed and bound in Great Britain by
Windsor Print Production Ltd, Tonbridge, Kent

CONTENTS

PREFACE

No book can remain up to date with a fast-moving industry such as the print media. Magazines come and go, often out of the blue, even though launches no longer proliferate as they did in the last few decades of the previous century. In these more cautious and financially stringent days, magazine publishers tend to reinvigorate their existing and less successful titles with buzz-words such as 'new look' and 'refocus' (jargon for 'What the hell can we do with the tired old thing?') or else lethargically produce a 'me-too' following a currently fashionable formula.

Newspapers also move more slowly in these times and are less likely to give us sudden surprises. The buccaneering days of the past are, largely, behind us, but the battle goes on. Some of the flamboyant personalities who bestrode Fleet Street have themselves 'gone to press' (or prison).

I have been a print obsessive all my adult life. My appetite was originally whetted by a favourite aunt who, when I was about twelve, presented me for Christmas with a book by Cecil Hunt called *Ink in My Veins*. I resolved to get into Fleet Street when I grew up. But I was destined to grow up rather quicker than my parents and school envisaged. War broke out, my father was called up, and I had to leave school at fifteen. I got a job on a weekly shipping magazine: not exactly green eye-shields at dawn, but I wallowed in the reporting assignments, layouts, proofreading and subbing. After three years with His Majesty, mostly involved in scriptwriting and announcing with Forces Radio in Italy and Vienna, I made it to Fleet Street, not as an editor, reporter or sub but in the advertising world of the *London Evening News*. Still, it was Fleet Street!

After that I enjoyed a long and happy life in magazines from the then affluent *Farmers Weekly* and the innovative *New Scientist* to the glossies and the launch of *Harper's & Queen*, *Cosmopolitan* and *Country Living*.

In the list of further reading at the end of this book I acknowledge some of the works that have helped me to recall some of the post-war history of the newspaper industry, and the list can provide those interested with fascinating background material on the people and events in the Street. Fortunately newspaper people love writing about newspapers. For a definitive history in meticulous detail over the years I recommend the book *300 Years of Fleet Street* by Dennis Griffiths, published by the London Press Club in 2002 to commemorate the 300th anniversary of the first newspaper with an impressive ceremony at St Bride's Church in Fleet Street attended by the industry's great and good.

In this book I have been critical – and probably annoyingly opinionated – about elements of the present world of newspapers and magazines. But the criticism comes heartfelt from a devotee of the medium. I voice my concern at the new and – to me – alien practice of giving away newspapers, not because I am against the idea of getting newspapers into the hands of people who otherwise wouldn't bother to buy them but because I fear these free papers are creating a lazy reading habit. The evening give-aways seem so superficial. They merely present a series of soundbites and advertorial which can often be read between single stops on the London Underground. There is no editorial commentary or in-depth news. I fear that instead of steering would-be readers towards better newspapers they may well do the opposite.

Newspapers have a hard road ahead in the face of electronic competition. Circulations are generally falling, classified advertisements are increasingly available online, and the young are devoted to the internet. The habit of newspaper reading is in decline all over the world. *The Times* recently reported that the French now buy just 167 newspapers per 1,000 people, compared to 263 per 1,000 in the USA. In the UK we buy 393 per 1,000, but for how long?

I also abhor the celebrity culture, fuelled by the raft of magazines exploiting tittle-tattle about the famous and those who are famous for being famous, putative celebrities and fame's mayflies. The whole fashionable obsession with celebrity has spread inexorably into the red-top tabloids and even the broadsheets. Gossip may drive circulation, but it also puts the grubbiness into Grub Street.

If you can hear the thunderous sound of hoofs as you read this book it is the galloping of my hobby-horses! Give-away evening papers, celebrity tosh, lads' mags that think their editorial ethos should be 'getting your kit off for the boys', overweight weekend papers, Page 3 girls, newspaper bingo – these are just a few of my least favourite things.

I leave you with the familiar street cry: 'Readallabahtit!'

1

THE WAR AND THE 1950S

DECADES OF RECORD CIRCULATIONS

–

THE CORONATION, USHERING IN THE CULTURE OF
THE ROYAL SOAP OPERA

–

PICTURE POST

–

THE ARRIVAL OF COMMERCIAL TV AND THE DEATH
OF THE BIG NATIONAL WEEKLIES

–

THE WITHDRAWAL OF KEMSLEY FROM NEWSPAPERS
AND THE ENTRY OF ROY THOMSON

This is a book about newspapers and magazines, the print media which for five hundred years have educated, entertained, exploited, sensationalized and scandalized, in the process constantly reinventing themselves. Throats have been cut, reputations created and ruined, fortunes made and lost. It is a story with heroes and villains. We all love the Press and we all hate the Press. This is a book about 'then' and 'now', about an industry which is frequently vilified and sometimes even praised. It is about an industry which is often slow to react to advanced technology but which has an innate ability to survive – and prosper.

From the time that Wynkyn de Worde set up his printing press in Fleet Street in 1500 and William Rastell operated his printing and publishing company in St Bride's Churchyard in 1530, the newspaper industry has seized every opportunity to flourish and develop in an atmosphere of often tigerish competition. The first daily newspaper was the *Daily Courant* in 1702, and Edward Cave first used the word 'magazine' in 1731 when he launched the *Gentleman's Magazine*.

The Education Act of 1870 brought elementary education to children of all classes, producing a massive increase in literacy, and the development of the railways created a more peripatetic population with the time and opportunity to travel – and hence read books, magazines and newspapers. A series of tax changes on paper and advertising and new printing processes opened the way for an avalanche of new magazines and the development of the daily and regional press.

The Victorians were quick to exploit the new technology, seizing the chance to reach vast new readerships. The *Guardian,* the *News of the World*, the *Daily Telegraph*, the *People*, the *Financial Times* and the *Daily Mail* were all Victorian creations, while *The Times* and the *Observer* date from the previous century. Magazines can claim even earlier parentage, with the *Tatler* being founded in 1709 and the *Spectator* in 1711.

Victorian ladies loved magazines that featured society gossip, fashion and household hints and were the first to appreciate the intriguing new art of the agony aunt. After the Great War the middle classes found themselves with fewer servants or none at all, so their owners welcomed new magazines that offered them household hints and information about the conduct of domestic life.

By 1939, in the absence of television, newsreels, newspapers and radio were people's only sources of information about the war. However, many of the pre-war magazines faded away during the war years because of the rationing of paper, which continued until the 1950s. Some titles streamlined their editorial content to suit their considerably reduced size, and print orders were, at best, frozen at pre-war levels. But every copy of every popular magazine was grabbed off the bookstalls, and newspapers rapidly sold out, despite their reduced pages.

The war gave the women's magazines the opportunity to represent the Home Front to their readers, women left behind to look after their families, grappling with the problems caused by the bombing, food rationing and the constant demands that they salvage whatever they could, that they 'make do and mend'. *Picture Post* and *Illustrated* photographed the war on all fronts, while the big-selling national titles *Everybody's*, *John Bull* and *Punch* provided the lighter side. The men's titles, popular with the Forces, were *Lilliput*, *London Opinion* and *Men Only*, which must have been dog-eared by the time they had passed from hand to hand, from barrack room to barrack room.

This was a boom time for the printed media; the publishers' tragedy was their inability to exploit all the proffered advertising. The government insisted on more than its fair share of space to bolster their campaigns on food recipes, blackout regulations, Dig for Victory, National Savings, clothes rationing and much else, leaving a shortage of space for commercial advertisements. The Ministry of Food extolled the virtues of the 'new salt fish: as you know, it has to be soaked for at least twenty-four hours to get the salt out', and offered mouth-watering recipes for cod pancakes, salt fish Lyonnaise and baked cod with parsnip balls. The Ministry of Fuel thundered: 'Five pounds of coal saved every day by 1.5 million homes will provide enough fuel to build a destroyer.' The National Savings Committee was unambivalent: 'Buy nothing for your personal pleasure, or comfort, use no transport, call on no labour – unless urgent necessity compels. To be free with your money today is not a merit. It is contemptible. To watch every penny shows your will to win.'

The newspaper industry, which was to see such turbulence in the last forty years of the century, had enjoyed a relatively tranquil existence in the 1930s, at least as far as ownership changes were concerned. The merger of the *Morning Post* with the *Daily Telegraph* in 1937 cemented the latter's dominance of the middle-class market for many years to come.

The early days of the war, however, saw the *Daily Worker* suppressed in 1941. The *Daily Mirror* also famously received a yellow card from the Prime Minister in 1942, narrowly avoiding closure. The offence was caused by a political cartoon by Philip Zec showing a torpedoed sailor on a raft in an empty sea with the caption 'The price of petrol has been increased by one penny – official'. I remember my parents' indignation at the cartoon. The wrath of the Home Secretary, Herbert Morrison, descended on the paper, and the Editor was commanded to report to the Home Office to be severely censured ('to get a bollocking', the *Sun* would surely declare today). However, the newspaper's fortunes were hardly dented by the incident. In 1941 its circulation stood at 1.7 million, and later it would average 4.6 million. It was dubbed 'the Forces Paper' during the war. Moreover, since its launch by Alfred Harmsworth in 1903 it had always been popular with women. It was certainly *the* newspaper in my parents' house during the war and the austere year that followed. We loved the cartoons: Ruggles, Garth, Popeye and Captain Reilly-Foul. We enjoyed the Live Letters edited by the Old Codgers. And in my teenage years the undressed adventures of Jane were alluring.

For many years the star columnist of the *Mirror* was William Connor, who wrote under the pseudonym Cassandra. In 1941 he vehemently attacked P.G. Wodehouse for his broadcasts from Berlin after his capture in Le Touquet. My father, an ardent Wodehouse fan and an arch-critic of Cassandra's column, was furious. By a beautiful irony he was called up into the Army and sent to Tidworth in the same draft as William Connor. Also in the same intake was Frank Owen, Editor of the *Evening Standard*, quite well known in business by my father.

Connor returned to the *Mirror* after the war to resume his Cassandra column. Probably his most notorious attack was on Liberace, whom he suggested, or implied, was homosexual. Liberace took him to court and won the case, costing the *Mirror* £35,000 in damages and legal costs.

The post-war editorial genius of the *Mirror* was Hugh Cudlipp, an early school leaver from Penarth in South Wales. Impressively, his two brothers also became Fleet Street editors: Reg ran the *News of the World* and Percy the London *Evening Standard*. They came up the hard route from Penarth via provincial journalism. Some years ago Hugh told me a story from his early days on the *Penarth News*.

As a fresh-faced, eager cub reporter he had pulled off a particular scoop. Basking in his glory, he was delighted to be praised by the Editor, who asked him: 'How much do I pay you?'

'Two pounds a week, sir.'

'I'm glad!'

Once he reached Fleet Street his career was amazing. Aged nineteen he became Features Editor of the *Sunday Chronicle*, then the *Daily Mirror*. By twenty-four he was Editor of the *Sunday Pictorial*. After war service with *Union Jack*, the Forces' overseas newspaper, he returned to Fleet Street, becoming Editor-in-Chief of the *Mirror* and the *Sunday Pictorial* and eventually Chairman of the International Publishing Corporation (IPC).

The *Mirror* was never backward in coming forward. In the 1950s it was particularly hectoring, as this front page proclaimed:

> *WAKE UP BRITAIN!*
> *WE'RE LIVING IN THE PAST*
> *WE'RE TOO SLOW*
> *TOO DAMN SMUG!*

This blessed plot, this earth, this realm, this England is not the place it was. This sceptred isle is deluding itself. This happy breed is backward. When the rest of the world uses words like 'Stuck in a Rut', 'Bumbling', 'Outdated', it is no longer talking about a Balkan principality or a South American banana republic. It is talking about Britain. About us.

The magazine industry was slow to energize itself after the war, but a first stirring came in 1949 when the National Magazine Company, the British end of the American Hearst Corporation, decided to launch *Vanity Fair*, a title aimed at young women. The magazine could claim to be the first major British magazine targeting young women with a fashion interest. The teenager had not yet been 'invented' or recognized as a separate breed; that was a phenomenon only discovered in 1960. The *Vanity Fair* reader probably dressed like her mother when she was a bit younger. Printed by photogravure, the magazine was an immediate hit with its target readership and was warmly welcomed by fashion companies that were beginning to establish themselves with the new post-war generation. The magazine's launch was an adventurous challenge to the post-war gloom in which so many of the surviving magazines looked dowdy and tired and were probably printed by letterpress. *Vanity Fair's* success spawned a crop of rivals in the ensuing years. Its circulation peaked at about 260,000 in the mid-1950s but was declining by the time it was closed by National Magazines in 1972 when the successful *Cosmopolitan* was launched . The fortunes of that magazine still fly high today on both sides of the Atlantic.

By 1950 the *News of the World*, the Sunday newspaper that used to be famous for relating the escapades of unfrocked vicars, perverse scoutmasters, absconding rural deans and general inappropriate hanky-panky, had built a circulation which has never been rivalled by a competitor, and it is extremely unlikely that it ever will be. In the peak years its sales topped a staggering 8.5 million, a tribute to its editorial skill in fascinating its readers every Sunday with endless accounts of prurient court cases. These days such stories would probably draw a yawn from the reader, but back in 1950 they offered a salacious peep-show for a wide-eyed readership of suburban curtain-twitchers. It was another seventeen years before it adopted a tabloid format after being purchased by the ambitious and acquisitive Australian Rupert Murdoch.

Circulation directors can only look with awe and envy at the circulations achieved back in the glory days of weak or non-existent competition. The *Radio Times*, standing proud and isolated as the only source of detailed programme information for the BBC's exclusive broadcasting service, sold over 8 million copies every week. Today it struggles, at a mere 1 million copies, to remain the third largest sale with six immediate rivals selling 4 million copies between them.

It was into this world of mega-circulations and massive readerships that I arrived in 1948, replete with my ill-fitting demob suit (grey herringbone) and pork-pie hat (blue). I joined the advertisement staff of the London *Evening News*, exhilarated with the buzz of Fleet Street to be a very small cog in one of the mighty empires which ruled the newspaper industry. The *Evening News* dominated the London evening market, selling a record 1.75 million copies every night. The first edition went to bed at about 8.30 a.m. and could be replated up to six editions during the day. It was also published on Saturdays and bank holidays. The expansive circulation was partly achieved by an impressive geographical reach, extending from the Wash round the south of London to Torquay. Looking back, there did seem to be a better service from your newspaper in those days. The replated editions kept up to date with the day's racing, for example, by printing the latest results in the fudge, the technical term for the now long-forgotten 'stop press' on the back page of the paper.

The London evening market was vibrant. The *Evening Standard*, then part of the Beaverbrook empire, sold 750,000 copies, and the *Star* from the *News Chronicle* stable sold 1 million. Londoners hurrying home to the suburbs and beyond were regaled with the old news-vendor cry of 'Starnewstandard!'

One of my regular jobs in my early training days at the *News* was the early shift on the 'copy desk'. This included collecting any last-minute changes to the advertisements or new blocks which had been delivered overnight and then hurrying to the printing building across the road. I still vividly remember the febrile atmosphere in that busy hall half full of linotype operators clattering out their metal print. The hapless advertisement man had to arrive at the 'stone', the centre of the printing operation, and report to the none-too-pleased head compositor with the changes demanded by the advertiser at such a late hour before the flongs were cast and the printing machines roared into life. I am sure many a young trainee in such a situation can recall the admonishment when asking for an alteration to a slug of type: 'It's not made of bloody rubber, sonny!' I might add that a fellow tyro on the day that we both began on the copy desk was a chap called Vere Harmsworth, whose subsequent promotion was somewhat brisker than mine.

In those far-off days the advertising was drastically limited as the *News* could only run six- or eight-page papers. We kept drawers full of copy blocks waiting their turn, often forlornly, to be taken out and their three-by-two column advertisement given the honour of actually running in the next day's paper. The classified department had similar problems with overwhelming demand. A solution was found by splitting the run, with two separate editions every day so the advertisers benefited only from half the circulation for their small ads. But the estate agents and secondhand car dealers rarely complained – they were only too happy to make an appearance at all.

The *News* was part of the *Daily Mail* troupe, which included the *Sunday Dispatch*. The odd one out of this collection was a strange and alien survivor from pre-war days. The *Continental Daily Mail* once flourished as a convenient newspaper for the idle and wealthy émigrés who resided in Paris or on the Riviera. The paper was still printed in Paris in the late 1940s and early 1950s with its own paper ration and edited by Noel Barber, later to be a successful novelist. The *Mail* exploited the ample advertising capacity by endeavouring to present it as a daily newspaper for British industrial advertisers to a supposedly eager continental audience of export buyers. It published endless 'special supplements' on a ragbag of subjects which might fast-talk some advertisers into buying space. Under the advertising energy of a Northcliffe executive, Jack Reeves, the paper employed a staff of some dozen eager young salesmen hoping to be promoted to a proper newspaper. The advertisers were assumed to be influenced by the *Daily Mail* name and reputation and were sometimes confused about exactly where they were buying space. During my thankfully short tenure on the paper we were ordered to speak personally on the phone to twenty managing directors a day to sell them space. The exaggerations and sales tactics employed by the sales force would bring a flush to the cheeks of the present-day management at Northcliffe House. Another tactic was to hire some 'C' list celebrity to tour the Ideal Home Exhibition and be photographed on the stand of a company that had agreed to buy advertising space. Not the *Mail's* finest hour.

In 1947 an event occurred that was fundamentally to influence the women's magazines and the red-tops for ever. The wedding of Princess Elizabeth to Philip Mountbatten was the first colourful celebration after the war. This was still a period of severe austerity, rationing and bomb damage, so the glitter and glamour of the wedding in Westminster Abbey came like manna from heaven to the magazines and the popular press. The wedding, and the birth of Prince Charles in 1948, were launchpads for a cornucopia of royal coverage that has since never abated. How grateful the editors of the women's weeklies must have been after the dark rigours of six years of war. The Liz/Phil industry burst on to the publishing scene to be exploited and done to death for the next sixty years.

The women's weekly market was then dominated by two titles: *Woman* and *Woman's Own*. These were the *grandes dames* and enjoyed breathtaking circulations: *Woman* sold 1 million and *Woman's Own* 750,000. These figures would soon be dwarfed by their later expansion, with *Woman* reaching 3.2 million and *Woman's Own* 2.5 million. These circulations are remarkable by contemporary standards and even more impressive considering the formidable competition in the 1960s when the two magazines were at their peak. There were ten weekly magazines aiming at the popular mid-market and many monthlies.

The emancipation gap between the Victorian young lady and the post-war *Woman's Own* reader is obviously extensive, but the gap between the 1950s and today is even more remarkable. In the 1950s the dominant theme in the big-selling weekly magazines was still the domestic lifestyle. A girl grew up, worked for a bit, got married, left her job and had children. Working mothers were not the norm, certainly not in the middle classes. Evelyn Home, who answered letters in *Woman's Own*, was still advising that once a woman had a family she was more contented in the home than working outside it. The Perfect Wife was the Perfect Housewife. A look through the advertising pages of the time assumed that readers cleaned, sewed, washed and looked after children. You can see Doris Day look-alikes enthusiastically radiating from the advertisements.

Cooking and recipes were staple features of the magazines. When *Woman's Own* ran a survey to establish the character of typical young British women, their favourite pastimes were found to be dancing, knitting, reading and sewing. Only a third smoked, and half were non-drinkers. The magazine was delighted to discover that 80 per cent of their respondents viewed marriage as their supreme ambition. However, times were changing. In 1958 the Queen called an end to the tradition of presenting débutantes to the Court; and female university entrants doubled in twenty years. Car manufacturers showed an incomplete grasp of the new reality: they conducted their own survey and announced that women were not directly involved in the process of choosing the make or model of the family car but might have an opinion about the colour.

Big changes in the newspaper business began in 1952 when Lord Kemsley decided to reduce his empire and relinquished some titles. He began by selling the *Daily Graphic* to Rothermere (who relaunched the paper as the *Daily Sketch*) and then merged the *Sunday Chronicle* and the *Empire News*. He sold the *Daily Dispatch* to the Cadbury family, who absorbed it into their *News Chronicle* as a circulation booster. Lastly, he sold the *Daily Record* to the *Daily Mirror*. He was also seduced by the notion of moving into the nascent commercial television industry, then up for grabs to the top buyer; he thought of twinning the franchise for weekend broadcasting in the lucrative Midlands with the North of England. But he then lost his nerve and withdrew his application. However, he retained his ownership of the *Sunday Times* for a number of years before selling to the myopic, good-natured and immensely shrewd Canadian Roy Thomson.

The royal boom was continuing to sell newspapers and magazines, with the Coronation in 1953 helping to break all records. The great British public, until then unconvinced about television, went out in unparalleled numbers to purchase sets so they could sit on their sofas and watch the glittering occasion in glorious black and white. The newspapers also benefited: the *Daily Mirror* sold 7,164,704 copies on Coronation Day, a record for a British daily newspaper.

In the same year Roy Thomson purchased the *Scotsman*, acquiring his first foothold in the British market where he was to make such an impact.

The National Magazine Company, owners of the British editions of *Good Housekeeping* and *Harper's Bazaar*, launched another version of an American title with *House Beautiful*. This was not a success, eventually folding into *Good Housekeeping* in 1968. But they scored a hit with the home-grown *She*, a new-style monthly edited by the television personality Nancy Spain. She broke new editorial ground with her cheerful and irreverent hotchpotch magazine with its tendency towards the quirky and sometimes scatological. In a format reminiscent of *Picture Post* and costing a modest shilling, it set out to be controversial and fun. It succeeded in both. Later it was to run extracts from Dr David Reuben's best-selling book *Everything You Wanted to Know about Sex* and a sexually explicit column by Doctor Devlin with his monthly features Organ of the Month and Position of the Month. This was raunchy stuff for the period. The formula of cheekiness, broad humour and sexual frankness was a big hit with the audience of housewives. Tragically Nancy Spain died in an air crash on the way to the Grand National in 1964.

Nothing better illustrates the booming advertising market of the 1950s than the strategic decision by both Odhams and Newnes, the rival magazine colossi, to launch two more weekly women's magazines. Odhams added *Woman's Realm* to its stable, and Newnes launched *Woman's Day*. The launches were clearly marketing-led: the intention was to benefit from the colour advertising that was being rejected by *Woman* and *Woman's Own*, which had both reached their optimum size. The new weeklies were launched with planned circulations of 1 million, which would appeal to major advertisers but also attract less wealthy companies seeking colour impact but finding the big titles unaffordable. The cover price of both new entrants was a modest fivepence, but *Woman's Day* never made the grade because it had too few fresh editorial ideas, was rather mumsy and failed to excite. Even Barbara Cartland's Agony Aunt page could do nothing for the title, and it was ditched in 1961. *Woman's Realm* fared better, surviving all the way into the new century, expiring from exhaustion in 2001.

The year 1956 saw the Hungarian revolution, the Suez crisis and the return of petrol rationing. This was probably not the most propitious time to launch a new national weekly magazine, but plans had been laid for the introduction of the *New Scientist*. A new publishing company had been formed, headed by Maxwell Raison who had been in the forefront of Hulton's *Picture Post* in 1938. Raison had retired from publishing but had been stirred by Winston Churchill's call for industry to understand and communicate with science and vice versa. The new magazine was edited by Percy Cudlipp, formerly of the *Daily Herald* and *Evening Standard*, and printed on newsprint to give it urgency and economy. It soon established a weekly sale of 50,000 copies. I joined the company for the launch. Our advertising efforts were considerably assisted by the current national enthusiasm for new technology and the fast-developing nuclear industry. This was the time of 'prestige' advertising: all the monolithic corporations so prevalent in those days were major advertisers in the new magazine, not only to blow their own corporate trumpets but to attract university graduates to join their burgeoning staffs. The technology boom also created a welcome need for many pages of classified advertising for staff. In short, *New Scientist* was a magazine waiting to happen.

Percy Cudlipp was a brilliant choice as Editor. The magazine also had a Science Editor, Tom Margerison, an egghead who later left the magazine for a successful career in commercial television. Cudlipp was the man who made the magazine headlines, running relevant features and luring his past newspaper contacts into writing for the magazine. During one of those transport strikes in the 1950s, which seemed to be more regular than the trains, I used to pick up Cudlipp every morning, on my drive up from Richmond, from his house in Holland Park and take him to our Holborn office. The journey took an aeon through the strike-bound traffic, and it gave me a wonderful opportunity to listen to his views on life in general and newspapers in particular. He was more serious in demeanour than his brother Hugh but a gifted raconteur with amusing and incisive views on our profession.

In 1960 we followed *New Scientist* with the launch of a sister magazine *New Society*, with the intention of achieving in the social sciences what the former had done so effectively with technology. However, the new venture failed to attract sufficient display advertising and was eventually taken over by the *Guardian* as a supplement. Maxwell Raison, a self-effacing but shrewd businessman, was bought out by IPC, and *New Scientist* was moved into Reed Elsevier, where it flourishes to this day.

Commercial television arrived in September 1955. How intrigued we were when a commercial for SR toothpaste flashed on to our black-and-white screens. The new medium was disdainfully dismissed by the press, which was understandably protective of its vested interests. But the shock of the new medium proved to be a smack in the eye for the popular general magazines. Edward Hulton's *Picture Post*, *John Bull*, *Illustrated* and *Everybody's* soon bit the dust. These sad deaths reflected the American experience when the giant weeklies *Look*, *Life* and *Saturday Evening Post* fell like cut timber, unable to match the sheer audience numbers of the new enemy.

The loss of *Picture Post* was particularly poignant, although its demise had undertones of family politics to add to the advertising and readership decline. Out went the splendid and flamboyant magazine that had carried us through the war years with memorable journalistic and photographic reports and after the war with incisive social comment. Tom Hopkinson, the Editor through most of the magazine's greatest years, recalled in his introduction to *Picture Post 1938–1950*, after the magazine's demise in 1957, the editorial ethos which had made it so successful:

> *Picture Post*, for a great part of its life, applied itself to the issues which most concerned the young and thoughtful people of its time. Such issues were dealt with far less adequately in the rest of the forties and fifties than they would be today. There was virtually no television. *Picture Post* thus became, for millions of young men and women, the magazine which handled the subjects they talked and argued about amongst themselves. Equally, in my time as editor, I was never happy unless I could see in every issue some topic which was going to be discussed and argued over. I was convinced that in order to survive the magazine had to be provocative and controversial.

Picture Post was never chary of being controversial. A typical feature in 1949 asked:

> Is there a British colour bar? Britain stages Colonial Month – a campaign to stimulate popular interest in the life of the people and the Colonies. The King attends the opening ceremony. But there are more than 20,000 Colonial people who live amongst us. What do we know of them – of their work, of their living conditions, their hopes and grievances? *Picture Post* conducts a survey into this dangerous and important question.

This led to a six-page feature shot by Bert Hardy in Liverpool, Cardiff and London. The lead photograph was shot on a Liverpool pavement.

> A coloured British subject expresses the indignation of his people: officially there is no colour bar in Britain. But restaurant keepers and landladies, employers and employees, even the man in the street, says Nathaniel Ajayi, he and his people meet with considerable colour prejudice. Ajayi has lived in five European countries, was a British prisoner-of-war in Germany, but says he knows of no European country where the coloured man is treated with more unofficial contempt than in Britain.

In 1949 this was tough talking, and tough journalism, about a subject largely ignored by the rest of the press and the public. No wonder *Picture Post* was missed.

John Bull had been launched in Edwardian times by the notorious Horatio Bottomley, the editor and Liberal MP. He fell from grace when sentenced in 1922 to seven years' penal servitude for issuing bogus Victory bonds. The magazine's printers had always been Odhams, and on the departure of Bottomley it took over the publishing responsibility, running the title until its closure. *Everybody's* was pure entertainment, edited by the splendidly named Greville Poke. *Illustrated* was a photo-journalism weekly, again from Odhams, which never attained the stature of *Picture Post*. *John Bull* moved into the 1950s with drawn front covers in the style of the American Norman Rockwell covers on *Saturday Evening Post*, amusing and rather folksy everyday situations. Towards the end of its life the magazine was merged into *Illustrated*, but its demise was only postponed. Dentists' waiting-rooms lost another staple.

The magazines cost only fourpence a copy, but the market was intensely price sensitive. In 1955 *Picture Post* took the plunge and increased its cover price to sixpence; the public reaction was immediate and punitive, and within weeks the price was reduced back to fourpence. Marketing was tough for these general titles. *Picture Post* occasionally ran three-dimensional photographs which could only be viewed wearing special glasses provided with the publication. Members of the Hulton staff were encouraged by the management to get out the magazine and the spectacles when travelling by bus or tube and look amazed at the novelty. I do not remember that this had much effect – except that we must have looked pretty bizarre.

From Hulton Press came the legendary boys' comic magazine *Eagle*. The Reverend Marcus Morris, an ambitious vicar from Southport, had touted the concept of a more serious and quality comic around London publishers without success, but the Board of Hultons were immediately impressed by his layouts and originality and gave him the go-ahead to publish. *Eagle* was a brilliant mix of Bible stories, comic cartoon strips and explanatory cut-outs of technical icons such as the London double-decker bus, ships and submarines. But the undoubted success of *Eagle* came from the cover story by Frank Hampson featuring Dan Dare, Pilot of the Future. The magazine's formula was so successful that Hulton and Morris followed it with *Girl, Robin* and *Swift*. *Girl* carried the adventures of Kitty Hawke, an airline pilot with an all-girl crew, and a nursing story, Susan of St Bride's. The comics put on the Hulton Boys' and Girls' Exhibition at Olympia for a number of years. In its heyday the circulation of *Eagle* topped the million mark. By the 1960s, when the comic was owned by IPC, the editorial concept changed, featuring front covers of Marty Wilde and Billy Fury.

In 1959 Kemsley surprised Fleet Street by selling his newspaper interests to Roy Thomson, who had already successfully bid for the commercial television franchise in Scotland with his classic boast that it was a 'licence to print money'. To develop his interests north of the border Thomson had tried to purchase the *Press & Journal* from Kemsley but had twice been rebuffed. Now he was suddenly offered the complete Kemsley Group for the astonishing bargain price of £5 million. This risible sum made him the overnight owner of three national Sundays, thirteen provincial dailies, several weeklies and a provincial Sunday. He soon expanded the regional titles by founding evening newspapers, which used advanced technology, in Reading, Watford, Luton, Slough and Hounslow. All this and the *Sunday Times* in his pocket.

A sad demise in 1960 was the closure of the liberal *News Chronicle* and its London evening newspaper the *Star*. Dating back to 1930, an amalgamation of the *Daily News* and the *Daily Chronicle*, the daily had been launched and financed by the Cadbury family with Walter Layton as editorial director. After the war, during which Layton had been appointed by Churchill to the Ministry of Supply and the Ministry of Production, the paper's fortunes had declined, despite incorporating the *Daily Dispatch* in 1955. Layton thought the papers were 'hanging on by their eyebrows' financially, and the Cadbury family decided on closure. The death of the *Chronicle* also saw the departure of Richard Winnington, who many felt was the best film critic writing in the popular press. The *Star* was always the weakest of the three London evenings, despite selling 1 million copies a night.

During this period some of the most famous names in British magazine publishing disappeared. A takeover frenzy broke out in 1958 when the Mirror Group purchased Amalgamated Press, with its raft of women's titles, and renamed the company Fleetway. The following year Odhams Press took over Hultons and George Newnes. This created a merger of the two mega-rivals, placing under the same roof many competing titles such as *Woman* and *Woman's Own*,

Amateur Gardening and *Popular Gardening*, *Motor* and *Autocar*, *Ideal Home* and *Homes and Gardens*. Then in 1961 Odhams was swallowed by the Mirror Group, putting a whole bookstall's worth of magazines under the same commercial direction. Under the banner of the IPC the company moved to a skyscraper on the South Bank, quickly known to all and sundry as the Ministry of Magazines. Later IPC itself was handed over to Time Warner, transforming the largest chunk of the British magazine industry into an American colony.

While the magazine industry was indulging in this whirlwind of takeovers and mergers, the newspaper business was also about to enter a dramatic period of changes which would mould the industry for the rest of the century.

2

THE 1960S AND 1970S

The national Sunday press experienced changes as the 1960s opened. Roy Thomson, happy with his windfall deal from Kemsley, closed two of the acquisitions, the *Sunday Graphic* and the *Empire News*. Rothermere, suffering continuing losses with the *Sunday Dispatch*, a paper that had established a reputation for publishing bodice-ripping serials, closed the paper but sold the title itself to Beaverbrook. This was a useful boost to the *Sunday Express*, consolidating its domination of the middle-class Sunday market.

Roy Thomson had big ambitions for the *Sunday Times*. In 1962 he launched the paper's colour magazine, a first for Fleet Street, after installing new colour presses. Edited by Mark Boxer, lured from *Queen*, the new supplement was a style success and a major circulation booster. The creative agency people loved it, media buyers discovered its cost-effectiveness as a source of high-quality national colour, and the paid-for magazines sensed the arrival of an uncomfortable new competitor in the colour market. In cost-per-thousand terms it presented a formidable challenge, mopping up pages of cigarette, booze and car advertising. The main paper also introduced the Insight section, and, under the editorship of Harry Evans, the publication flourished. Sunday papers would never be the same again.

The magazine scored an early coup by appointing Lord Snowdon, a.k.a. Tony Armstrong-Jones, as 'Artistic Adviser' on a retainer of £5,000 a year plus fees for special assignments. His first contribution to the magazine featured Margot Fonteyn and Rudolf Nureyev, and over the years he produced many much-admired features. But he was poached by rival the *Telegraph Sunday Magazine* in 1989 with a contract of £35,000 a year plus another £35,000 for twelve assignments a year.

Hunter Davies was also to serve time as the Editor of the colour supplement. In 2008, on the death of the artist Beryl Cook, he recalled in the *Sunday Times* his pleasure at receiving some transparencies of paintings by the then unknown Cook. He thought they were charming and took them to the art department, who scathingly declared them boring, amateur and derivative. But Davies went ahead with the pictures and wrote a story to accompany them. His victory over the art department was enhanced by the purchase of one of the Cook originals for £10.

Fleet Street can never be left behind when a good idea arrives, and the *Observer* and the *Telegraph* were quick to launch their own magazines. The *Telegraph* began with a Friday publication but soon moved to Sundays. The popular Sundays were more cautious, although some were to fall in line over the years. While I was a director of *Queen* magazine, Jocelyn Stevens was hired by Max Aitken of Express Newspapers to develop new editorial ideas. Jocelyn and I set up a series of meetings with several top media directors of the advertising agencies to seek their views on a proposed *Express* magazine. We asked each of them the pertinent question: Which day of the week would you recommend for publication? Their answers were confusing: Thursday, Friday, Saturday and Sunday!

Meanwhile the world of magazines was also undergoing a revolution. The 'teenager' was invented. No longer just 'young adults', the new breed was being recognized as a substantial new market. Dr Mark Abrahams, of the leading advertising agency London Press Exchange, defined the teenager as 'a person who is aged thirteen to nineteen unless he or she happens to get married before'. The sudden realization that there were 7.5 million people aged between twelve and twenty-four in the market was an exploitation opportunity not to be missed. The estimates were mouth-watering: 7 million teenagers spending £3 million each day.

First off the starting block was *Honey*, published by Fleetway. *Honey* was aimed at the archetypical 'new' girl: affluent, trendy, spending a lot on cosmetics, perfumes and fashion. Launched with the slogan 'Young, gay and go-ahead', the magazine set the pace, and rival publishers reacted in the traditional way – they jumped on the bandwagon. Out came a troupe of titles: *19, Petticoat, Boyfriend* and *Trend*. Up in Scotland D.C. Thompson, home of *Dandy* and *Beano* and the 'comfy press' with *People's Friend* (1869) and *My Weekly* (1910), caught the teenage fever with *Blue Jeans, Jackie, Patches* and *Red Letter*. The teenagers were spoilt for choice, and the publishers reaped their rewards.

The year 1964 introduced to the popular magazine world a distribution novelty that came to dominate the market for many years. It first took off in America, where Cowles Communications launched a magazine entitled *Family Circle* which could be bought only in the supermarkets. Sainsbury's in the UK had already placed a cautious toe in the exclusive availability market with its own title *Family*. The content was aimed at the housewife (who else went food shopping in 1964?), and it tried to look like a conventional woman's magazine with general 'housewifey' features. All the food credits acknowledged only Sainsbury's. Today it looks rather limp and grey, not a title that could lead a marketing revolution.

Into the picture stepped Roy Thomson, ever the opportunist, who recognized the potential for magazine sales in the burgeoning supermarket sector (then a pygmy compared to today's mammoth), particularly if he could seize the exclusive rights. He entered the arena with a joint ownership deal with Cowles, later buying them out. He negotiated to supply the supermarkets with his own version of *Family Circle*. Sainsbury's represented a stumbling-block because of the conflict with its own *Family* but agreed to merge their title into *Family Circle* in return for the privilege of providing Sainsbury's supplements within the new magazine. At the same time Thomson brought out another minor supermarket title, *Trio*.

Surprisingly, from today's perspective, the Thomson deal stayed solid for twenty-five years. This was the period of sensational, if controversial, expansion of the supermarket sector, with Tesco, Asda and Sainsbury's vying to open ever bigger and better stores. And when you visited your local supermarket at the checkout was your exclusive *Family Circle*. Sales of the magazine peaked at 1 million copies, a hitherto unheard-of circulation for a woman's monthly magazine. At the risk of disturbing or offending the shade of Lord Thompson I have to record that the wholesale trade (which had been cut out of the deal) cast doubts on the authenticity of the sales figures, as distribution was carried out by Thomson's teams, who were responsible for supplying and topping up copies in the stores as well as reporting the sales figures – not quite the standard of national audit one would expect these days. In 1967 the success of this distribution deal was reinforced with the introduction of *Living*, which set out to represent 'lifestyle' rather than the kitchen or the larder.

What a deal this was! In retrospect it seems that the other publishers were paralysed by its success, incapable of breaking the arrangement and apparently unable to grasp the enormous potential of the supermarkets' footfall. Although the editorial style of *Family Circle* and *Living* could be rather plodding, they were popular with shoppers as they shuffled along the queues at the checkouts, picking them up along with last-minute supplies of tissues and sweets. And advertisers found them a powerful vehicle for publicizing the goods that were sold in the stores.

Thomson's luck had to run out eventually, however. Tesco began to sell other magazines in a slightly haphazard manner, 'cherry-picking' the best-sellers. The powerful IPC also began to sneak in its top women's weeklies at some of the checkouts. Indeed it was to IPC that Thomson sold his two magazines in 1988, correctly anticipating the demise of the monopolistic arrangement. By this time the pattern of magazine and newspaper distribution was undergoing fundamental change.

The year 1964 saw another new dawn. The *Daily Herald* had been launched in 1912 as the official organ of the Labour Party, printed by Odhams. Fortune did not smile on the paper. In 1922 a new alliance of the party and the TUC took control, but the *Herald* continue to lose money, and Odhams, which already held over half the shares, assumed full ownership. By 1964 Odhams, now merged into IPC, decided that the paper needed a new look, a new dress and a new title to survive in the intense competitive heat of the popular dailies. The result was the birth of the broadsheet version of the *Sun*.

The new title was not a success; it was still losing substantial sums of money after a disappointing launch. But it caught the eye of a new contender, a man who came to play an egregious role in Fleet Street's fortunes. Robert Maxwell, Labour MP for Buckingham and owner of the Oxford-based scientific Pergamon Press, attempted to purchase the *Sun*. He planned to relaunch it as a tabloid which would be printed on the *Evening Standard's* presses at night. But he had previously been thwarted by Rupert Murdoch when he had made a play to buy the *News of the World*, and it was Murdoch who gained control of the *Sun*.

The new-style *Sun* appeared in 1969, edited by Larry Lamb. It garnered a million sales within a few weeks, although it was not until 1978 that it outstripped the *Mirror*. Lamb had picked his editorial staff skilfully, and he included a women's section headed by the experienced Joyce Hopkirk, later to be launch editor of *Cosmopolitan*. The Lamb formula included lots of sports coverage, plenty of women's interest and always bright, breezy and smart front-page headlines. And, of course, there were the famous page 3 girls with their immodest display of mammaries and cheerful smiles. Murdoch had clearly won the centre ground with his new big-selling daily combined with his still risqué *News of the World*. A new era had arrived, kick-started by the transformation of the poor old workers' workhorse back in 1964.

Murdoch's *Sun* quickly attained a reputation for cheekiness and humour. It gave the world unforgettable front-page headlines such as 'Freddie Starr ate my hamster' and the shamelessly xenophobic 'Up yours Delors!' and 'Hop off you frog!'

Lamb was a man with a mission. I met him once in the early days of his editorship and rather stupidly remarked, 'The pundits seem to be knocking you.' His reply was justifiably withering: 'Don't read the pundits. Read the paper!' His successor was Kelvin McKenzie, who launched the successful bingo wars of the 1980s, playing with budgets that enabled the paper to reach jackpot prizes of £1 million.

The death of Lord Beaverbrook in 1964 marked the beginning of the end of a newspaper epoch. Max Aitken, born in Canada in 1911, had very successfully plunged into various business interests as a young entrepreneur, eventually emerging as one of Canada's richest men. He arrived in England in 1910, was to become a Liberal Unionist MP and was knighted in 1911. His mercurial jet-propelled career flourished during the First World War, when he became the Minister of Information and a Privy Councillor. He was given a baronetcy by Lloyd George in 1917.

He launched the *Sunday Express* in 1918 with no immediate success; the circulation soon dropped to half the launch figure, and the losses after two years stood at £500,000. In a complex series of deals involving Lord Rothermere and Edward Hulton, he acquired the London *Evening Standard* and by 1932 he controlled the *Daily Express*.

From this point he moved at the speed of light, hiring the best talents. He eschewed any extension of his business into the provinces, concentrating on the development of the *Daily* and *Sunday Express*.

It is impossible to comment on the successful *Express* story without extolling the influential role of Arthur Christiansen, Editor from 1933 until 1956 when he suffered a heart attack. He had profoundly impressed Beaverbrook while working as assistant editor of the *Sunday Express*, when he scooped the rest of Fleet Street with his instant reporting of the disastrous crash of the airship R101. By the mid-1930s the *Express* was riding high with a circulation of 2,200,000, claimed to be the highest in the world. Christiansen was helped by Beaverbrook's tactic of employing a network of reporters to cover all the world's major events. The paper was not without its critics, particularly the Prime Minister Stanley Baldwin who strongly resented its constant attacks on him and his policies.

After the Second World War, during which Beaverbrook had taken a full role in Churchill's War Cabinet, the two *Express* papers continued to win the circulation battle in Fleet Street. The Sunday paper was selling 3 million copies and the daily 4 million. But the 1960s saw a severe setback in the company's fortunes, with critics suggesting that the policy of owning only two national papers should have been supplanted by a move into the regional press or an investment in commercial television. The newspapers' plant was becoming obsolete, and the new *Sun* and the *Daily Mail* were offering severe competition. The management, along with the rest of the industry, desperately wanted to move from letterpress to new technology but was constantly frustrated by the unions. Losses mounted and circulations sagged. Even with the fresher energies of Max Aitken and Jocelyn Stevens the *Express* newspapers were never to recapture the authority and circulation performance they had once known.

After Beaverbrook's death the group was run by his son Max Aitken, a wartime fighter pilot who eschewed his title, declaring that there would only be one Lord Beaverbrook in Fleet Street.

Younger readers may be surprised to learn that it was as late as 1966 that *The Times* moved news to the front page. Up to then this precious position had been occupied by a full page of classified advertising. In the same year the Astor family sold the newspaper, together with its supplements, to the now powerful Roy Thomson.

While the merry-go-round of national newspaper ownership continued to spin, the magazine industry was also moving and shaking. IPC unloaded its Napoleonic chairman, Cecil King, in 1967, and by 1975 the Reed Group had split into separate groups, Mirror Group Newspapers and IPC Magazines. The goliath of the periodicals industry needed to display some creativity and invention. One of its earliest moves was the appointment of Clive Irving from the *Sunday Times* as Editorial Director with creative responsibilities for the entire group, charged with the awesome task of creating new magazines that would meet the demands of new audiences thirsty for fresh ideas. Out went the tired old formulae, supplanted by an exciting approach to the coming and more affluent generation.

Irving's first editorial challenge was to revive *Woman's Mirror*, an ailing Sunday newspaper for women that had already been converted into a weekly magazine. Sales had slipped below 1 million (which compared unfavourably with the competing IPC weeklies), and the advertising agencies could hear its death rattle. Irving wrote in the trade press: 'What is happening in *Woman's Mirror* is a good indication of how we see the future woman's market.' The formula his team introduced was to shock and sensationalize. An early issue carried a front cover picture of a foetus, an inside story illustrating the development of an embryo in the mother's womb. That issue sold out in a few days, but the publishers were perhaps moving too fast for the magazine's intended public and they closed it when its sales figures were down to 850,000 – a figure which sounds very respectable today.

Much more successful was the launch of *Nova* in 1965, published by Newnes as 'the New Magazine for the New Kind of Woman'. After a shaky start, involving a change of Editor after only two issues, the title hit its stride. It owed much to the brilliant art direction of Harry Peccinotti, who produced striking front covers and original layouts. The editorial ethos was forthright:

> Twenty-eight or thirty-eight, single with a job or married with children . . . A girl with a university degree, or a girl who never took school seriously. The social permutations are endless. What remains constant is that our kind of woman has a wide range of interests, an inquiring mind and an independent outlook . . . Not to mention that her numbers are multiplying. What is there for a woman to read? At Newnes, we believe that she is hungry for a magazine of her own, one that looks at life from her own attitude

and ranges over many interests. *Nova* is not an implied criticism of existing magazines, but an assertion of the emergence of readers with new requirements.

And the readers were out there – the circulation quickly soared to 150,000, much to the chagrin of the opposition. I ran the advertising for *Queen* during the early *Nova* years, and the newcomer's circulation was an embarrassment to us with our slimmer 50,000 sale. The advertising agencies loved the new title; they admired the revolutionary editorial ideas and the adventurousness of some of the page layouts. The photography was stunning and the editorial sexy, sometimes bordering on dubious taste for the times.

Nova had found a new image, neither housewifey nor glossy, and attracted devoted readers. It certainly made many other titles aimed at women look dowdy and distinctly old hat. But this success did not last. There were changes of editorship, and the magazine began to lose its edge. The ABC figures started to show six-monthly drops in circulation, and the shock tactics the magazine often employed produced a reaction among advertisers and readers. The page size was reduced to A4 (the launch size had been almost 'coffee table') and eventually to A5, pocket-sized.

Meanwhile the ethos of other women's magazines had begun to change: titles became more sexy and unconventional, taking much of the gloss off *Nova*. And in 1972 *Cosmopolitan* was launched with spectacular success, another body blow for the ailing *Nova*, which finally succumbed when the circulation hit a low of 86,000. The magazine was closed, a sad end to an original, exciting and bold publishing venture. A senior executive at Newnes reported that the magazine had never made a profit over its ten years of publishing. In hindsight, *Nova* was a great publishing idea ruined by successive editors.

Meanwhile on the newspaper front there was a development when the *Daily Mail* absorbed its decidedly sick sister paper the *Daily Sketch* and converted to tabloid format in 1971. Three years later Fleet Street suffered another shock when *The Times* moved from its historic offices in Printing House Square to the more dowdy Gray's Inn Road. Some old hands suggested satirically that the next move would be for the paper to go tabloid.

Back in 1860 a young and ambitious Samuel Beeton, publishing husband of Mrs B. of *Household Management* fame, launched a society journal named *The Queen*, having received the gracious permission of Her Majesty to use the title. The journal meandered along as a fashion and society periodical, but it was looking pretty tired when it was purchased by Jocelyn Stevens, nephew of Edward Hulton, in 1957. Stevens had been raised by his uncle, having lost his mother in childbirth. Steeped in the atmosphere of publishing, he had worked at Hulton Press after Cambridge, and on his twenty-fifth birthday, when he came into his inheritance, he bought *The Queen* (soon dropping *The*). It was a strategic purchase: the exciting sixties were around the corner. Stevens transformed *Queen* into a trendy, relevant magazine exactly attuned to the current mood of entrepreneurial energy and innovation. He hired an impressive cast of journalists and photographers. His art director was Mark Boxer, and his photographers included Patrick Lichfield and Anthony Armstrong-Jones. Quentin Crewe wrote the uncompromising and witty restaurant reviews, Elizabeth Smart did the book reviews, Anthony Burgess assessed new long-playing records, Brian Inglis discussed medicine, Cyril Ray was the wine correspondent and Clement Freud was 'Mr Smith', an anonymous investigative figure. The motoring page was written by Stirling Moss. Another Stevens coup was to purloin Betty Kenward from *Tatler* as Society Editor – she penned the famous, if often turgid, 'Jennifer's Diary' for many years. The magazine's circulation never exceeded

50,000, but in those happy pre-ABC circulation days that didn't matter. What *did* matter was cachet, panache and style. The product was the thing, and advertisers scrambled to get into those glossy, 'with-it' pages.

The editorial was often socially irreverent and frequently controversial. Stevens himself became a sought-after media figure: handsome, golden-haired and wealthy. He acquired a reputation for being difficult and fussy (or perfectionist) and was often bombastic in his relations with editorial staff and sometimes with the advertisers. There were wild stories of his tendency to defenestrate, notably the rumour that he threw his desk out of his fourth-floor office window. It was all exaggeration. In my five years as a fellow director I can only recall one such incident . . . and that was just a telephone!

It was not always sweetness and light with Jocelyn. Inefficiency angered him at times, and a Stevens anger outburst was wondrous to behold. We used to run a regular feature called 'In and Out', praising the 'Ins' and seeing off the 'Outs'. In one issue Harrods, an important *Queen* advertiser, was declared 'Out'. A ton of bricks fell on my head as advertising director from a furious Scottish managing director (Harrods was the House of Fraser in those days). I tried to placate him, but he insisted on talking directly to Jocelyn as Editor. I transferred the call and rushed upstairs to Jocelyn's office, expecting to listen to him soothing the aggrieved director. As I arrived I heard a great bellow: 'Why don't you just fuck off back to Scotland!' Harrods advertisements did not appear in *Queen* for some time.

Later Jocelyn declined an offer to become Editorial Director of IPC Magazines. It would have been great: a raging bull on the rampage in the placid meadows of the Ministry of Magazines. (Many years later he was to create cathartic mayhem at the Royal College of Art and English Heritage.) Instead he joined the *Express* group as personal assistant to Max Aitken, quickly becoming Managing

Director of the *Evening Standard*. He achieved a Fleet Street first on 21 July 1969 when he put out a full-colour edition of the *Standard* on the moon landing, produced largely twenty-four hours before the event but on sale when London went to work the morning the news broke.

The Editor of the *Standard* was Charles Wintour and he and Jocelyn enjoyed a prestigious and financial partnership, achieving a big increase in classified advertising and introducing full colour, which was much used by classified advertisers. It is still relatively rare in newspaper production.

Jocelyn became Managing Director of the *Daily Express* in 1972 and was closely involved in the proposed merger between Associated Newspapers and the Beaverbrook Group. The merger was a real possibility until two suitors arrived, hair brushed and carrying bouquets. One was Rupert Murdoch; the other, more surprisingly, was Trafalgar House, run by Nigel Broakes. Trafalgar House was an international conglomerate active in shipping, with the Cunard Line, the Ritz Hotel and extensive civil engineering interests.

It was Trafalgar House who won the day, renaming the newspaper group Express Newspapers, thereby eliminating the Beaverbrook connection and dynasty. The chairman of the new group was Victor Matthews, later to be Lord Matthews. The new company looked for expansion, resulting in the launch in 1978 of the *Daily Star*, the first new national newspaper launch for seventy-five years. The *Star* was printed in Manchester and produced by facsimile in London. The Editor-in-Chief was Derek Jameson, a cockney lad full of bouncy charm. He led the *Star* into a bingo war against the *Sun* and the *Daily Mirror* with a first prize of £1 million. Jameson was a firm believer that bingo was a more valuable circulation builder than the editorial content of the paper. He was later to be made Editor of the *Daily Express*, whereupon *Private Eye* dubbed it 'Tits by Christmas!', suggesting that semi-nudity would help circulation against the *Sun*. The group was sold by Trafalgar House to United Newspapers in October 1985, but this was not to be the end of the *Express* saga.

In 1976 Britain's oldest Sunday newspaper, the *Observer* (which first appeared in 1791), sold its majority shareholding to Atlantic Richfield. Tiny Rowland, perhaps best remembered these days for his feud with Mohammed Al-Fayed of Harrods, acquired the paper but sold it to the Guardian Media Group in 1992. The paper went on to set a Fleet Street record: four editors in five years.

The late 1970s were marred by a wave of national strikes. The year 1976 saw the beginning of fourteen months of a bitter dispute involving the workers of the Grunwick photo-processing factory in Willesden, north-west London. The owner, George Ward, had refused to recognize the trade union APEX, and half the workforce, about 150 workers, went on strike. They were all sacked, resulting in one of the biggest trade-union disputes of the decade, with flying pickets and secondary strikes. Clashes with the police and many arrests constantly made the headlines and the news bulletins, but George Ward's right not to recognize the union was upheld in the House of Lords.

The dispute was finally settled in 1978, the year in which publication of *The Times* and the *Sunday Times* was suspended for a painful twelve months. This was a Luddite moment – the print unions refused to use the new machines installed in the basement print plant in Gray's Inn Road, the Thomson headquarters. Eric James, a *Sunday Times* staff member, gives a blow-by-blow account of this extraordinary year-long hiatus in the history of two of Britain's greatest newspapers in his book *Stop Press*. In fact, 1978 was a year of labour disputes across the industry owing to the unions' resentment at falling behind in national pay-scales after years of government-imposed pay restrictions, although their pay settlements were generous in comparison with many other industries. At the heart of the unrest was the proposed introduction of electronic technology, which was viewed by the workforce as a major threat to jobs and working conditions at all levels.

As a magazine publisher, with no direct link with the print unions except as a client, I was always intrigued by the generous wages paid by the big newspapers to their printing staff, particularly when it came to part-time shift work. For many of the printers employed by the company we contracted to print our weekly *New Scientist* Christmas came every week. They came up from the suburbs to Fleet Street to work freelance on the late printing of the Sunday newspapers. The money they received was reputedly bountiful in proportion to their usual weekly wages. They clocked in under pseudonyms, such as Mickey Mouse or Elvis Presley, to preserve their anonymity and avoid the attentions of the Inland Revenue. According to one or two less discreet employees, they often skived during those Saturday night shifts, becoming skilled at card games in preference to the unsavoury labour involved in machine minding.

The Times had hiccupped along through 1978 with the loss of occasional issues. The management, led by the Chief Executive Marmaduke Hussey (another alumnus of the *Daily Mail* copy desk in my day there), played a strict and tough game, which was understandable as the losses began to mount up. In the first quarter of the year they lost £2 million in revenue, frequently failing to reach the full quota of a night run of the paper. The loss of readers and advertisers was unacceptable to the owners, and after many management–union meetings the crunch came in November. The result was a total shutdown of *The Times*, the *Sunday Times*, the *Times Literary Supplement* and two educational supplements, a shattering blow to the Editors, William Rees-Mogg of *The Times* and Harold Evans of the *Sunday* and to the entire business revenue machine. The dispute dragged on until

November 1979, resulting in mammoth losses to the company, and even then the 'new technology' problem was still not resolved.

Strikes can also affect the magazine industry, even though they seldom own their own print facilities. In 1959, when the finances of *New Scientist* were at a critical point, the print unions took nationwide industrial action, totally shutting down our printers, but we cleverly – we thought – anticipated the problem, for it would have been devastating to us to lose even one issue. The management negotiated with a private company in Dusseldorf to take over our printing during the strike. In hindsight this was a short-sighted step. The international brotherhood of trade unions bore down heavily on the Germans, who consequently stopped printing our magazine. This presented us with a double problem: not only did we stand to lose production but we had already sent over the whole issue's galleys of type and printing blocks, and they now sat idle in Germany. A colleague, who spoke reasonable German, and I flew over, located our printer in Dusseldorf and commandeered our material. We hired a delighted taxi driver to drive us to Calais in his Mercedes with the boot and much of the back seat bulging with our metal. At Calais we bribed the purser of the cross-channel ferry to allow us on board with our hefty load. We arrived at Dover next morning, and a Customs official asked if we had anything to declare. 'Just these,' we replied, pointing to six burly porters each pushing a trolley laden with our galleys and blocks. An hour later, after much consternation and head-scratching over the rule book, the Customs officials allowed us to proceed into Dover where a colleague waited in his large car. In our absence a non-union house had been discovered 'somewhere in England' and the magazine was saved.

This was not my last adventure in strike-bound Europe. After the launch of *Cosmopolitan* we could find no suitable British printer able to handle our print runs (now reaching 600,000) and sought a photogravure printer abroad. The most impressive was Burda, the giant publisher and printer in Bavaria. This became a successful partnership. Copies of the magazine travelled by truck from Offenburg to Sveningen in Holland and then over to the container port in Felixstowe. They were then driven to Banbury for eventual distribution.

All went well until the Dutch dockers went on strike. An entire issue lay in containers at the Dutch port and the dock union leaders were adamant that there was to be no movement until their strike was settled with the government. I went off to Holland and had a pleasant meeting with amiable strikers in their flower-bestrewed caravan on the dockside, a congenial encounter lubricated with glasses of Heineken. But they were obdurate. I returned to Schiphol airport and telephoned Franz Burda, head of the printing operation. His immediate reaction was they would reprint the entire issue and send the copies over by air to Banbury. This was an astounding offer: the cost was staggering, but Burda insisted that the charges were down to him and he would send over two executives to discuss the logistics. However, the very next morning, while we were in a meeting with the Burda executives, we were telephoned to say the strike was over and the containers were already on their way. This was a telling example of how continental printing companies were winning British magazine contracts at the time. We also printed *She* in Italy. There were no strike problems there, but an entire consignment of one month's edition was severely delayed when the truck driver spent the night with his *innamorata* somewhere on the journey across Europe and the lorry was stolen during the night!

The saddest newspaper closure came in 1980 with the sinking of the London *Evening News*, the only broadsheet evening paper in the capital. Sales and advertising had been in decline, and even though the *News* retained a bigger circulation than its only rival, the *Evening Standard*, its fate was finally sealed by the failure of merger talks between Associated Newspapers and Beaverbrook.

But now important events were under way. First came the launch of the *Mail on Sunday*. (The publishers were prevented from using the obvious title, the *Sunday Mail*, because the name was already in use in Scotland.) Although this newspaper was not a success in its early days, I note it as a milestone because it was the first national newspaper to be photo-composed. At around the same time came the merger of the print unions that were to play a major role in the future development of the British press. The National Graphical Association (NGA) absorbed the Society of Lithographic Artists, Designers and Process Workers (SLADE), the Society of Graphical and Allied Trades (SOGAT) took in the National Society of Operative Printers and Assistants (NATSOPA).

However, the most headline-grabbing event had occurred the year before: Rupert Murdoch purchased *The Times* and the *Sunday Times* from Lord Thomson. On the face of it, Thomson was relieved and Murdoch delighted, but the Australian owner of the *News of the World* and the 'soaraway' *Sun* also inherited Fleet Street's perennial problems of over-manning, restrictive practices, huge overtime demands, last-minute pay demands and, of course, the lingering reluctance to modernize with new computerized machinery.

Readers may puzzle why Rupert Murdoch was permitted to buy *The Times* and the *Sunday Times* without an extensive investigation by the Monopolies Commission. In fact the deal was waved through by the government. John Biffen, Conservative Trade Minister, told the House of Commons that the delay which would be created by holding such an enquiry would risk the permanent closure of *The Times*. (Discuss!)

Turning to the world of magazines, we have noted that in 1972 National Magazines had lobbed a bombshell into the women's market with *Cosmopolitan*, the British version of Helen Gurley Brown's runaway American success. I was the launch publisher.

Although we were excited to be launching such a successful import on to the British market, there were serious doubts as to whether we could find the same 'Cosmo girl' as in the United States. Our first research was not reassuring: the research company came up with the statistic that British women were not over-eager to be taught about sex by an American woman. And our circulation forecasts were considered to be over-optimistic. No other younger women's magazine was selling as many as 100,000 copies by the end of 1971. Our advertising rates were based on a guaranteed sale of 150,000 with the rash promise of rebates if that figure was not reached.

The pre-launch publicity for *Cosmopolitan* was extensive. Newspapers and television constantly heralded the new magazine, creating an excitement that led the news trade to keep updating their sales forecasts and orders. In the event, the first print order of 350,000 was a complete sell-out by lunchtime on launch day, and the second issue had a sell-out figure of 450,000. These print runs were unprecedented. Excitement was undoubtedly generated by the promised feature of a male nude in the second issue, which today sounds lame but which in 1972 caused a minor sensation.

Given the national problems that the government faced in 1972 – the miners' strike, struggles in Northern Ireland, the 'cod wars' with Iceland, and entry into the European Economic Community – it is bizarre to recall the bad-tempered brawl that took place between the government and *Cosmopolitan*. The government's Prices and Income Board were behaving with irrational intransigence. Companies were forbidden to increase the prices of their products . . . full stop. We had launched *Cosmopolitan* with an advertisement rate based on 150,000 copies. The soaraway success of the magazine's circulation gave us print orders and monthly sales far in excess of that figure. Advertisers who had booked space in the magazine were enjoying a windfall. Naturally we increased our rate card to a more realistic figure for future bookings. Enter the Bad Fairy, the Prices and Incomes Board, to say 'no price rises'. This was a laughably impossible situation commercially. Marcus Morris (of *Eagle* fame and now Managing Director of National Magazines) had a personal confrontation with Geoffrey Howe, the minister responsible for the policy. Howe was obdurate: no price rise was permissible. The very logical argument put in simple terms which we thought a minister might comprehend – that the original price was for a pound bag of potatoes and that bag now contained three pounds – was pooh-poohed. Our prices were not to be increased. But we put up our rates none the less, with the approval of the advertisers and their agencies, as they all wanted to buy space in *Cosmopolitan*. A Man from the Ministry arrived at our office, threatening death by hanging, drawing and quartering and, even worse, legal action. The company was taken to the High Court as an example to British commerce, for we were the only company being thus pilloried. We were found guilty as charged and ordered to return all the money acquired from the rate rise. The agencies were horrified: they had already taken their commission on space which had appeared and been paid for. We were full of gloom and fears that the future of the magazine was in doubt. Enter once more the Man from the Ministry. 'Just trying to prove a point!' he told us – ensuring that the dignity of the law was upheld. We were then permitted to charge the new rates, and there was no requirement to refund any revenue. After all, he said, it was a very logical price rise! This was hardly an attack on the freedom of the press but a salutary reminder that civil servants should not interfere with market forces.

The *Cosmopolitan* story is now a publishing legend, and until the launch of Condé Nast's *Glamour* no rival came within a mile of Cosmo's success. The formula has been replicated all over the world in nearly forty editions; the Hearst Corporation has enjoyed a sub-industry of joint ventures with overseas publishers.

Although the magazine is now thirty-six years old, arthritic by some standards in the ephemeral magazine game, it still retains a high circulation and a readership of young women whose mothers probably bought the first issue. *Glamour* now outsells it but without the same readership reach.

Cosmopolitan's striking and immediate success had a detrimental effect on the young women's magazine market. *Vanity Fair*, the 1949 pioneer, was immediately closed by National Magazines, followed rapidly by the deaths of *Flair* and *Modern Woman*. *Cosmo* was also a body blow to *Nova*, which staggered on for three more years before being folded by Newnes.

In the same year as *Cosmo, Spare Rib* appeared, which described itself as a 'woman's liberation magazine'. It was the antithesis of *Cosmopolitan*: unglossy, uncommercial, radical, feminist and political. It carried no mainstream display advertising but featured classified notices for folk festivals, political rallies and feminist events. *Spare Rib* none the less survived for twenty years, a tribute to its uncompromising and honest commitment to the feminist cause, driven by the Editor Rosie Boycott who went on to edit the *Daily Express*.

What could IPC in the new climate? It held, of course, the middle ground of the women's market with its two big weeklies and a host of more specialized titles. It now launched *Candida*, pricing it at 10p. The going rate in those days for a weekly was 8p. I always thought that the choice of the title itself was unfortunate: apart from the Shavian 'new woman' implication, candida is a parasitic, yeast-like fungus which can cause thrush. Raising disapproving eyebrows at *Cosmo's* vulgarity, *Candida* was designed to appeal to a more sober woman: 'stimulating company, joyous, interested, vital, intelligent and impatient'. The magazine suffered a tragedy with the sudden death of its Editor; it failed to click and was closed in the launch year. And if that was a quick demise IPC's first issue of *First Lady* broke a record. The launch issue was printed and publicized, but, because of the financial climate and the three-day week in 1974, the launch was postponed and the title never surfaced again.

Bob Guccione, who had established *Penthouse*, the men's 'skin' magazine, tried in 1974 to move into the female market with *Viva*, published on both sides of the Atlantic. The fashion editor was Anna Wintour, later to be dubbed 'Nuclear Wintour' when she would appear for *Vogue* at fashion events invariably wearing dark glasses. The magazine featured overt nudity, causing W.H. Smith to refuse to stock it, hastening its early death in 1979.

Company was offered by National Magazines in 1978 in an attempt to emulate the success of stablemate *Cosmopolitan*. It gained a successful foothold but in later years went rather too far for many tastes towards a sexual agenda.

Many a Fleet Street tycoon, and many an editor, has dreamed of emulating the massive American successes, *Time* and *Newsweek*, by launching a political and news magazine in this country. In 1979 Sir James Goldsmith, wealthy and forthright in his political views, chanced his arm by launching *Now!*, replete with the exclamation mark which was to feature strongly with the later arrival of celebrity magazines. But *Now!* had a tough time of it, being welcomed by many advertisers but failing badly on the circulation front. In a fool-hardy move, one most publishers tend to avoid, he publicly vowed to return money to his advertisers if his circulation failed to achieve the promised levels. The circulation failed to oblige, and Goldsmith returned chunks of money and withdrew the magazine.

Enter Robert Maxwell once again into the Fleet Street fray with his purchase of Mirror Group Newspapers from Reed International for £113 million. This threw him immediately into the front rank of Fleet Street proprietors, as he now owned not only the *Mirror* but the *Daily Record* in Scotland and three Sundays: the *Sunday Mirror*, the *People* and Scotland's *Sunday Mail*. The racing paper *Sporting Life* was also part of the package. Reed had battled the print unions for years in an attempt to convert their papers to the new technology. Maxwell was more successful, which prompted him to endeavour to expand his empire. He judged there was an opportunity for a new London evening newspaper, as the field was now a monopoly for the *Evening Standard*, which was now wholly owned by the Daily Mail Group. He launched his *London Daily News* in February 1987 at a price of 20p. However, in a cunning strategy Rothermere brought the *Evening News* back from the grave at half the price of Maxwell's new paper as well as reducing the price of the *Standard* itself. Maxwell was forced to cut his price to 10p, but the *Evening News* slashed its price to 5p. Maxwell was outgunned and had to close his new paper in July. This was an interesting foretaste of the 2008 battles on the London evening paper front – even if the new publications are street give-aways.

Another new appearance in 1978 was *Faces* from Marshall Cavendish, better known for a series of part works, which were very popular in those days. *Faces* was a weekly attempting to capture the market that *People* had reached in the United States, but the magazine suffered from a run of bad luck. The editorial staff, members of the National Union of Journalists, went on strike, resulting in SOGAT blacking the title, seriously affecting the sale of the first four issues. When the magazine regained distribution it was unfortunate that the front cover picture happened to be the same one as was used on the cover of that week's *Woman's Realm*, which did not help sales. The publishers aimed for a circulation of 300,000 but probably achieved only about half that figure. The magazine was closed after thirteen unlucky issues.

Many of us in the women's magazine press at the time of the departure of *Faces* were sure that a weekly based on personalities would never succeed in this country. We pontificated that the population was too small to provide enough subject matter and stories to fill fifty-two issues a year; pop stars, television soap stars, royalty, a few philandering politicians perhaps, but hardly enough headline superstars to fill all those pages and to find front-cover subjects. Maybe we were naïve, but we were still some years away from the floodtide of so-called celebrities that later engulfed the popular media. We were, I suppose, a bit like the unfortunate Hollywood tycoon who dismissed the proposal for a movie of *Gone with the Wind* as just another Civil War film.

3

THE 1980S

THE FLEET STREET DISPERSAL

–

EDDY SHAH AND *TODAY*

–

THE LAUNCH OF THE *INDEPENDENT*

–

CONRAD BLACK AT THE *DAILY TELEGRAPH*

–

THE BATTLE OF WAPPING

–

THE GERMAN INVASION OF
THE MAGAZINE MARKET

–

THE ARRIVAL OF *HELLO!*

The 1980s were a decade of momentous change in the restless newspaper industry. Two old houses were to see ownership changes, and Fleet Street itself experienced a historic dispersal. We have noted the purchase of *The Times* and the *Sunday Times* by Rupert Murdoch, and the rascally Robert Maxwell's achievement of his long-cherished goal of owning a leading national newspaper group – an event that would have considerable reverberations. But ownership changes were only one of the tremors to hit Fleet Street, which was beginning to face the unavoidable truth that its printing and production practices were outdated and uncompetitive.

However, there was good news on the sunny side of the Street. Two new national dailies were to be launched, one the harbinger of technological advance and the other a fresh breath of political attitude. On the other hand, in their wake came a new, semi-pornographic Sunday, tits swinging, to liven up the day of rest for the prurient.

The sale of Express Newspapers (now renamed Fleet Holdings via Trafalgar House) was particularly poignant to old hands in Fleet Street. We were very familiar with the impressive black glass building (the Black Lubyanka, as it was dubbed by *Private Eye*) and the daily arrival of gigantic rolls of newsprint delivered to the side of the building. Big changes had taken place since the great Beaverbrook days: the staff had been reduced to 1,700 from a high of 7,000, and the papers lacked their old zest and campaigning styles. The new owners were United Newspapers, run by Lord Stevens (David, not Jocelyn). Production was moved from Fleet Street to Docklands and the editorial offices moved across Blackfriars Bridge to a handsome riverside building. The editorship was a bit of a revolving door in the years leading up to the next change of ownership in 2000: Nicholas Lloyd, Richard Addis and Rosie Boycott were to occupy the chair in a three-year period.

Up the road from the Black Lubyanka stands the dignified edifice occupied by the *Daily Telegraph* for many years. Although its position as the organ of the middle and professional classes remained unchallenged, with a sale that usually dallied around the million mark, the *Telegraph* and its sister *Sunday* now began to feel an uncomfortably cold draught. They needed the 'new' technology, financing and new publishing blood to drive them forward in the looming battle with the Murdoch press. The papers were owned by the Berry family under Michael Berry, elevated to the title Lord Hartwell after the death of his father. His wife, Lady Pamela, had been a driving force in the family and the company, being an active and powerful socialite until her death in 1992.

Enter Conrad Black, Chairman of the Canadian company Hollinger Inc., who had made millions from the ownership of a chain of small newspapers across North America. With Rubert Hambro acting as go-between, Hartwell engineered a deal with Hollinger, to the displeasure of the Berry family. By 1986 Hollinger had acquired a majority shareholding, Max Hastings was appointed Editor of the *Daily Telegraph* and Peregrine Worsthorne of the *Sunday Telegraph*. At the beginning of 1987 the new plant at West Ferry in east London became operable, printing 1 million copies a day. The editorial offices left their stately Fleet Street building and moved to the Isle of Dogs, subsequently moving again to Canary Wharf and eventually Victoria, after more dramatic events.

For an investment of a reported £50 million Conrad Black had gained control of one of Britain's top newspapers, having bypassed and outwitted the possible purchasing ambitions of Mohammed Al-Fayed, Lord Hanson, United Newspapers and the Australian Fairfax. But he also inherited a loss of some £12 million when the newspaper's books were examined.

On the magazine front, Condé Nast took over *Tatler*, the glossy society journal, from the Australian publisher Gary Bogard. Before that it had been owned by the Illustrated Newspaper Group ('the Great Eight') run by Lord Thomson. Thomson closed the title in 1966 and relaunched the magazine briefly as *London Life* under the editorship of David Putnam, later to be the producer of the film *Chariots of Fire*. Putnam set out to make his magazine a trendy pacesetter, full of the buzz of the Swinging Sixties. It failed to attract enough advertising and readers, competing against the formidable *Queen*, and it took an early bath. Under the editorship of Tina Brown, backed by the Condé Nast publishing expertise, *Tatler* was now transformed and regained its former reputation as the glossy for the trendy, moneyed set.

The launch of a new fortnightly, *Just Seventeen*, in 1983 was a success for EMAP, which was already mining the young market with *Smash Hits*. EMAP, the acronym for East Midland Allied Press, had built up a solid reputation in regional newspapers across its area, and in 1950 had begun to exploit its newsprint printing facilities by inventing hobby weeklies in the fishing and motorcycling fields. The company's successful foray into the cut-throat world of women's magazines owed much to the flair and inspiration of the young David Hepworth, who was very much in tune with the contemporary mores of the young. *Just Seventeen* was launched as a 45p fortnightly, later to be promoted to weekly, backed by a major television campaign, and the first issue was banded free to *Smash Hits*. The editorial was a standard mix of fashion, personal problems, pin-ups, beauty features and pop music news. But the treatment was new and fresh, with fun layouts and jazzy graphics. Sales settled down to a respectable 200,000 in a notoriously fickle market.

EMAP continued to move confidently into the field of women's magazines, in competition with National Magazines and IPC. They launched *Elle, Looks, More, New Woman, Big!* and *Period Living* and later took over *Top Santé*. After a successful and ground-breaking career, *Smash Hits* closed in 2006, and *Just Seventeen* died after a desperate attempt to convert it to monthly publication as *J17* – it is usually a mistake to attempt to breathe new life into an expiring title by whittling the name down to initials (the name *J17* sounded like a medical formula for acne rather than a sexy icon for teenagers). But EMAP continued to develop its portfolio into new areas of female interest, publishing many successful magazines before surrendering its sovereignty to foreign invaders.

Back in the troubled world of national newspapers, Rupert Murdoch's patience and temper were being severely tested by the sheer obduracy of the print unions. News International was constantly beset by the outmoded problems of over-manning, last-minute demands for higher pay and restrictive practices in general, which all contributed to print shortfalls and missed deadlines. Murdoch decided that the solution was to build a new printing plant away from Fleet Street and recognizing a single union to represent all printing employees. The union he chose was the EETPU, the Electrical, Electronic Telecommunications and Plumbing Union, and the site of the new plant was Wapping, somewhere out in the East End – not conveniently sited for the traditional Fleet Street journalists' watering holes. This would be a comprehensive operation, complete with computerized typesetting facilities. It would also become the editorial and management offices for all the News International papers, *The Times, Sunday Times, News of the World* and *Sun*. A confidential contract was placed with a company called Atex for the typesetting; the unions knew Wapping was to be a print plant, but the typesetting arrangements were kept secret. Members of the EETPU were bussed to Wapping every day and the plant was being prepared for conflict, with a twelve-foot-high metal fence topped by razor wire.

The unions realized that they faced an intractable proprietor. They met News International executives and offered wide-ranging concessions over working practices and manning levels. But they were told that their members were not required at Wapping, and there were heavy staff losses. The anticipated strike followed, with 5,000 print workers taking industrial action. Meanwhile, all News International's journalists voted to go to Wapping. The print unions were broken, despite violent protests outside the plant and constant clashes with the police. Picketing continued for most of the year, but Murdoch had scored a crushing victory, much to the wonderment of executives throughout the print media world. The days of restrictive practices were over.

One evening I was shown around the new offices and plant by Charles Wilson, then Editor of *The Times*. I found the atmosphere quite astounding. Cheerful young workers in relaxed clothing and trainers were running the whole plant, right down to the distribution packing. And, even more surprising, Wilson told me that most of the jobs I saw were interchangeable at any time – not what my experience of newspaper and print plants had accustomed me to. The distribution arrangements for the plant were efficiently handled, with bundles of newspapers loaded from the bays on to TNT lorries. Trains were no longer required.

Murdoch's victory transformed not only the rest of the newspaper industry but every printing operation that magazine publishers dealt with.

Another notable date in Fleet Street's progress was 4 March 1986. A new national newspaper was launched – and by a non-Fleet Street man called Eddy Shah, who ran the Messenger Group of free newspapers in the Manchester area. Shah was committed to computer typesetting but had come into conflict with the typesetters' union, the NGA, when he decided to move his freesheets to Stockport. Refusing to acquiesce to the union's demand for a closed shop, Shah was confronted by 4,000 pickets attempting to prevent the *Messenger* publishing in Warrington. The use of 'flying pickets' was soon to be outlawed by the Thatcher government. Shah next set his sights on Fleet Street and national publishing. He proposed to publish a seven-day full-colour national newspaper, printed web offset at several satellite plants with direct input by the editorial staff. The title of his paper was *Today*. He raised £18 million for the venture and published the first issue on time.

Brian McArthur was the Editor and Jeremy Deedes Managing Editor. Jane Reed, hot from a brilliant editorial and business career at IPC, was appointed Features Editor, although Deedes was soon to leave to join the *Daily Telegraph*.

The new paper found the going unexpectedly tough, particularly on the circulation side, and when sales dropped to 400,000 new money was needed. Lonhro, the new owner of the *Observer*, invested £10 million and bought out the original shareholders for a further £10 million. Shah remained as Chairman.

Lonhro, however, found the continuing losses unsustainable. Robert Maxwell, looking to extend his national newspaper portfolio, made a bid of £10 million for the paper with £30 million of loan stock, but Rupert Murdoch won the newspaper with a bid of £38 million, Shah selling out his own holding. David Montgomery from the *News of the World* was appointed Editor. (An intervening Editor had been Dennis Hackett, formerly Editor of *Nova*.) But even with the Murdoch millions and the new plant at Wapping *Today* could only struggle along until its closure in 1995. Thus ended a truly pioneering attempt to break into Fleet Street. *Today* even won the Newspaper of the Year Award along the way. Shah was a brilliant catalyst, and with Murdoch's gritty determination and financial muscle he helped to move the business of national newspapers into a new age. He returned to Warrington, but after an unsuccessful launch with another local daily, the *Post*, he sold the Messenger Group and moved into television production. He later became a successful novelist.

However, another new national newspaper did survive and prosper. The launch of the *Independent* on 7 October 1986 was the brainchild of Andrew Whittam Smith, Matthew Symonds and Stephen Glover, all *Daily Telegraph* executives. The launch and the pre-launch were professionally sold to advertisers and agencies. Editorial staff were recruited from *The Times* and the *Sunday Times*.

The paper began as a broadsheet, backed by a heavy advertising campaign on television and posters, created by Saatchi and Saatchi. The teaser publicity 'We are. Are You?' set the scene and emphasized the political independence that was so essential to the paper's *raison d'être* and its strategy of picking up readers disillusioned with the main political parties. Within a year of the launch the paper's circulation had reached a satisfying 360,000. Its success was strongly emphasized by its readership profile of young ABC1s so appealing to the advertising industry. In 1990 the *Independent on Sunday* was launched, edited by Stephen Glover.

Financial difficulties led to the papers becoming jointly owned by the Mirror Group and Tony O'Reilly's Independent Newspapers. In 1998 O'Reilly bought out the Mirror Group and achieved sole ownership. The ins and outs, ups and downs of the *Independent* venture are described in detail in Stephen Glover's book *Paper Dreams*. Glover eventually left the company and currently writes as a pundit on the newspaper industry.

This was also one of the magazine sector's most inventive periods. There were some brilliant and enduring hits and some doleful failures. It was really the women's titles that were constantly exploring new territory or more often reinvigorating old and trusted ideas. In truth, women's magazines have a tendency to stick to the over-familiar, constantly recycling proven, if tired, formulae. Worse, many titles are interchangeable, and if a magazine gives up the ghost few tears are shed. The readers of the expired title will merely shrug off their loss and start purchasing a look-alike. If this seems harsh, look at some of the major launches coming from the principal publishing players in the 1980s.

Title	Owner	Launched	Died
A la Carte	IPC	1984	1989
BBC Good Food	BBC	1989	
Bella	Gruner and Jahr	1987	

Title	Owner	Launched	Died
Best	Bauer	1987	
Cachet	Cachet	1985	1986
Celebrity	D.C. Thomson	1986	1988
Chat	IPC	1985	
Clothes Show	BBC	1988	1997
Cooks' Weekly	GH Press	1984	1988
Country Living	IPC	1986	
Elle	Hachette	1985	
Elle Décor	Hachette	1989	
Essentials	IPC	1988	
Etcetera	D.C. Thomson	1985	1986
Fiz	Home and Law	1982	1985
Girl	IPC	1986	1990
Girl Monthly	IPC	1986	1988
Hair & Good Looks	IPC	1984	1989
Hello!	Hello! Ltd	1988	
House Beautiful	National Magazines	1989	1987
In-Store	IPC	1985	
Looks	EMAP	1985	2002
Marie Claire	IPC	1988	
Me	IPC	1989	1995
Mizz	IPC	1985	2006
More	EMAP	1988	
Options	IPC	1982	1999
New Woman	Murdoch	1988	2008
Prima	Gruner and Jahr	1986	
Rio	Link House	1981	1982
Riva	Carlton	1988	1988

Title	Owner	Launched	Died
Taste	Various	1986	1994
Working Woman	Wintour	1984	1987
World of Interiors	Condé Nast	1981	

Out of thirty-four start-ups, twenty have died, twelve in the decade of their launch. There are some positive successes, of course, in the table. The magazines launched by the German companies Bauer and Gruner and Jahr are still with us, and *Country Living* and its *doppelgänger Country Homes* are still healthy today. The French imports *Elle* and *Marie Claire* were proven successes in France for many years before the British editions arrived, and the Spanish *Hello!* was not only an instant success but was to establish a whole new sub-industry of magazines.

But what a restless decade! So many new magazines were pumped out into an already saturated market it was no surprise that so many met a quick end. Many were simply retreads, breaking no new ground – they filled no gap in the market, nor did they leave one.

At least the women's magazine had a go. There has been a dismal lack of original publishing ventures in the general publishing market. The only non-specialized magazine start-up worthy of discussion was *The Week*, currently published by Felix Dennis and selling a credit-able 150,000 copies. The concept from the start was uncomplicated – simply the pick of the week's news and comment from the national media both at home and across the world, including Best Articles: Britain and Best of the American Columnists. It is not above trivia: we are informed, for instance, of the eight discs chosen by the Castaway of the Week on the BBC's *Desert Island Discs*. The magazine carries 'talking points' from the newspapers, sport, the best letters (seem-ingly always picked from *The Times* and the *Telegraph*) and arts reviewed by its own critics. *The Week* is a clever project and is a useful bonus for busy people and those who might have been out of touch for a few days. Apart from the newspaper selection, it stands up well in its own right as an entertaining read. It is well presented and makes *Private Eye* look like a dishevelled auntie who never changes her clothes.

A magazine with a more political background is *Prospect*, a cerebral monthly much concerned with national politics and world affairs. Owned by an erstwhile Tory MP, Derek Coombs, it has achieved bookstall distribution as well as a healthy subscription base. It is not out to set the world on fire, but it stands out as an intelligent forum for debate.

Back in the Fleet Street hothouse, the nationals were still making their own domestic news. First, there were now women editors. Such an innovative phenomenon must have been regarded by some of the old hacks in their cosy local pubs, usually segregated by particular newspapers, as outrageous as the Church of England agonizingly arguing about women clergy and even contemplating the incredible idea of ordaining women bishops. But two such women made the Fleet Street grade: Wendy Henry of the *News of the World* and Eve Pollard at the *Sunday Mirror*. They were to be followed by Rosie Boycott at the *Daily Express* and Rebekah Wade at the *Sun*. Lori Miles was made Editor of the *News on Sunday*, financed by the trade unions and doomed to swift failure. But gender was no longer a barrier to the editorial chair.

Another development was the introduction of full-colour printing by the *Daily Mirror*, leading the way to more and more colour in the nationals, most useful as many of them were busy transforming their feature pages into women's magazines.

But the main story was the virtual death of Fleet Street itself as we all knew it. The Great Exodus had begun with Rupert Murdoch's controversial transfer to Wapping. Now the *Guardian* moved from the

Farringdon Road to Docklands and Associated Newspapers chose leafy Kensington as their new centre of business and editorial operations. By now the print revolution was complete. Electronic newsrooms, with direct journalistic input, were introduced, and printing was undertaken at satellite plants with electronically transmitted pages. The romance of the stone was dead. The keyboard was king.

Next to decamp was the *Express* which moved its editorial operation across the Thames and printed in Docklands. The *Telegraph*, *Observer* and *Financial Times* all moved away. The giants have all now left Fleet Street, which is a conglomeration of coffee bars, sandwich shops, mobile phone outlets, men's outfitters and other retailers. Ironically, W.H. Smith has closed its bookshop, leaving only two small kiosks to service the historic street of newspapers. Even Reuters has sold its august premises and moved to Canary Wharf. We have surrendered our homeland to the giant accountancy companies, with their bustling and urgent young employees who dash out of their offices to buy plastic cups of coffee and sandwiches before returning to their computers. Lunchtime O'Booze would be shattered. At least we still have the noble St Bride's, the journalists' church, which still sees hordes of Fleet Street personalities at the (seemingly ever more frequent) memorial services of erstwhile colleagues. Maybe Canary Wharf will eventually inherit Fleet Street's glamour and romance along with all the heartache, triumphs and sensationalism associated with the glory days of the Street of Ink.

Another aspirant newspaper tycoon emerged when David Sullivan launched the *Daily Sport* and the *Sunday Sport*. Outrageous, hugely fatuous, with pages of photographic 'glamour' (that is, topless women) and plenty of sports interest, the paper is unashamedly downmarket, appealing to the male footie fraternity. Sensational headlines have endeavoured to emulate the *Sun*. 'World War Two bomber found on the Moon' and 'Face of Jesus in my fish finger' come to mind. The paper also provided Sullivan with a medium for advertising his soft-porn magazines.

The magazine business has always lived with febrile competition, which in some ways is its very lifeblood. Magazines copy magazines, and occasionally – very occasionally – a bright new concept arrives on the bookstalls and leads the pack in a new direction. The British market has never been easy, but the competition was nearly always domestic. However, an aggressive new wave from Germany hit the business in 1987. The original attack was on the women's press, but in due course Teutonic tentacles spread across the wider magazine market.

We British publishers all knew our competitors, many of our editorial and advertising staff had worked for other companies, and inter-company intelligence was quite acute. We knew, or thought we knew, what was happening or going to happen in the business: start-ups, closures and makeovers. We were not used to foreign incursions, although an important chunk of our business was actually foreign owned. Decisions were ultimately made in New York for many of us. Most National Magazine and Condé Nast publications are British versions of successful American titles (*Vogue, Cosmopolitan, Good Housekeeping* and so on), but these were all part of the family somehow. But when the Germans launched their invasion of British publishing, and the women's market at that, it came like a bolt from the blue.

The first salvo to be fired was *Prima* from Gruner and Jahr, a giant German publisher seeking overseas expansion. It landed out of a bright, clear sky in August 1986. *Prima* had reached a 700,000 sale in Germany and a record 1.4 million in France; Britain was the next obvious area for development. The target readership was clear: women between the ages of twenty-five and fifty-four. The product was a classless monthly, very practical in content and representing good value for money. To the more sophisticated British market it seemed somewhat of a throwback – it did not trade on the newer mood of sexual freedom and raunchy transparency that had crept into our titles but concentrated on good, old-fashioned domestic content: lots of recipes, homecraft, beauty and health, knitting and sewing, childcare, pet welfare, travel and high-street fashion.

This was nothing to frighten the horses. However, Gruner and Jahr played one master stroke: at the very competitive cover price of 75p, each issue contained a paper sewing pattern, considered to be worth £1 alone. And on top of all this, G&J (as we grew to call them) had poached the experienced and excellent editor, Iris Burton, the editor of our own *Woman's Own*, to be the new editor of *Prima*.

G&J taught us a lesson in launching. I dubbed the invasion 'Panzer Publishing' with good reason, a reflection of their aggressive single-mindedness, blowing away all obstructions. Their launch advertising budget was a mouth-watering £1.5 million, using national television, commercial radio, the tabloids and 2,500 poster sites. (The entire budget for the launch of *Cosmopolitan* back in 1972 had been £127,000 to cover television, press, posters and trade advertising.) The result of this publicity blitzkrieg was a sell-out of the first issue of 450,000 copies, with the second issue scoring 650,000. We were gobsmacked. This very prosaic magazine would reach a million sale in the following year. We had to wonder just how valuable the paper pattern was and what contribution it had made to these record sales figures. (It was later quietly dropped.) Was the future to return to traditional family values? Had we been over-egging the trendy sexual pudding? Would every launch need a mega-advertising spend to make a dent in the market? A few optimists shrugged off the magazine's circulation as a fluke, which would swiftly settle down to a normal sale.

Little did we know that *Prima* was merely the vanguard of the invasion to follow. There were rumours that the Germans were planning a weekly. Publishers girded their loins and stood by to repel boarders. But there was no sign of a new magazine when many in the publishing business went off on their annual holidays. August is traditionally a quiet month, since readers are away on the Costa Brava and the distribution trade is in somnolent mood. Then on 12 August 1987 – when many publishers might be shooting grouse on a distant moor – *Best* arrived, the rumoured new weekly. It was modelled on G&J's *Femme Actuelle*, already successful on the Continent. There had been no trade presentations, no pitches to the advertising agency media departments. In fact, the trade's notice, given confidentially, had been a breathtakingly short two weeks. The traditional gestation period for a major magazine launch was customarily about six months, with plenty of fanfare and lots of trade parties. G&J made an announcement when *Best* appeared:

> One of the critical things about *Best* is the destiny. Our research showed that there is a measure of discontent with the weeklies and a feeling that they don't go far enough. Fun and entertainment are very important, but at the same time people want to be treated as grown-ups.

These unfamiliar sentiments must have reverberated through the corridors of IPC Magazines. The Editor was again Iris Burton, and *Best* was priced at an attractive 35p. It was devoid of much of the usual weekly mush: no 'knit your own Royal Family', no *Coronation Street* news, no gossipy features. Instead it had short, sharp, newsy stories, sound advice on money, legal rights and consumer affairs, health and careers. There were competitions galore and personality profiles. The household hints approach was left to the monthly *Prima* – *Best* was an information-stuffed 'good read'. Again, the circulation soon hit 1 million. *Campaign*, the weekly trade magazine, commented that 'Best was shaking up the meat and two veg approach in favour of a nouvelle magazine one.'

Bauer, a name which over the next twenty years would become very familiar to the British print media, did not intend to stand by and watch their compatriot competitors burst into the British market without launching their own incursion. They emulated the surprise tactic by rushing out Bella, a 29p weekly aimed directly at the IPC weeklies. With the slogan 'Something for Everyone Every Week' Bauer ploughed straight in with a familiar weekly formula: letters, health, gardening, knitting patterns, horoscopes, the Royal Family, sex problems, shopping, fiction, family doctor and so on. The target readership was younger than Prima's housewife, more the newly married. And they were not shy of the saucy or Rabelaisian, as an early letter attested: 'Whenever I get an erection, my wife has started calling me Concorde.'

The name Bella was chosen for the UK, according to a Bauer executive, 'because we want to get away from the plethora of titles in the UK called Woman's This or Woman's That, which all sounded the same. Bella was chosen as an all-purpose name with international credibility. It may be thought as Italian, but that doesn't bother us because the connotation is not negative.' Sales were slow, but a million copies were claimed, without the hindrance of an ABC figure (biannual circulation data from the Audit Bureau of Circulation).

Bella, Best and Prima gave the British magazine industry a wake-up call. They have faded considerably over time, dropping to a combined circulation of about 800,000 by 2008. But they were pioneers, and many other continental titles were to follow, with Bauer playing a considerable role in the market.

On the heels of the German successes, other foreign publishers were bound to look at the possibilities. Rupert Murdoch, not satisfied with mere newspapers, established Murdoch Magazines in the

UK with the launch of *New Woman*, an American title. The Editor, Frankie McGowan, went straight for *Cosmopolitan*'s jugular:

> A new woman is fun to be with, not a formidable challenge
> ... someone who is softer, more feminine than the myth of
> superwoman. We have come a long way since we were force-fed
> the illusion of that finger-snapping, high-flying executive in her
> power suit, pushing her way up the executive ladder while
> running the ideal home, perfect children and lover, fitting in
> aerobic classes on the side. No longer are we afraid to say that
> she is a figment of the media's imagination and nothing to
> do with us ...

So, Gurley Brown, you can't have it all!

However, the most far-reaching import was the Spanish *¡Hola!*, re-christened *Hello!* for the British market. This was something new to us, with its pages and pages of celebrity worship. The first issue in 1988 carried eighteen pages on the wedding of Burt Reynolds. Eighteen pages! This was a new brand of journalism – we would have covered the matrimonial story with one picture. But *Hello!* showed us how to squeeze the lemon to the very last drop: we had Burt up the aisle, signing the register, lighting a candle, showing the ring, kissing his wife, kissing his mother, kissing his horse, at the reception and off to this honeymoon by helicopter. Was this suited to the British palate? Not if early sales were anything to go by. None the less the arrival of *Hello!* opened the floodgates, and in poured an avalanche of me-too celebrity-worship titles.

4

MEN AND THEIR MAGAZINES

The market for men's magazines has been erratic over the years. After a long, dormant spell in the post-war period, during which all the old favourite humour titles kicked the publishing bucket, there was a sudden resurgence during the 1980s. This unexpected renaissance, which surprised the publishing business, uncovered a new sort of reader, very different from the old gin-and-tonic, Savile-Row-tailored leftover from the 'old days'. The two readerships could not have been more different in class, attitude or lifestyle. Out went 'gentlemen' and in came the lager-drinking, sporty, promiscuous, bird-pulling 'new lads', sometimes described as the 'educated yobs'. This affluent new social group was ripe for new magazines that would reflect their lifestyles and mores.

A magazine exclusively for men was not a new phenomenon. The very word 'magazine' had been coined by Edward Cave in 1731 with his *Gentleman's Magazine*, an instant success distributed in the ubiquitous coffee houses in the City. The magazine was laid out like a book, complete with a table of contents. There were columns such as 'A View of the Weekly Essays and Public Controversials', poetry, articles on witchcraft, lists of bankrupts, foreign affairs, a list of the new sheriffs, the season's fairs and classified advertising. Cave also pulled off a master stroke when he secured the journalistic services of Dr Samuel Johnson to write a series of pieces ridiculing parliamentary oratory. (We need you today, Dr J!)

Magazines went on to flood the Victorian market by the bucketload. Many, such as *Strand* and *Answers*, were bisexual in orientation. A strong competitor to *Answers* was *Titbits*, which offered a collection of peculiar incidents, unbelievable facts and oddities. (It was relaunched in the 1990s as a rather racy magazine for men, so the title was appropriate.) Other journals followed, with male readers in their sights: the *Gentlemen's Magazine, Man about Town*, the *Gentleman* and the *Gentleman's Journal*. They were all aimed at the top of the market, and reading them evokes a world of gaslight, stage-door Johnnies and hansom cabs. They tended to delight in excruciating jokes and puns, laboured jests that Mr Pooter would have appreciated.

The nineteenth century, during which the British Empire 'had grown and expanded at two acres a second', according to *Nash's Magazine* in 1902, witnessed a mammoth growth in the daily and weekly press. *Punch* had begun its long life in 1841, then *Vanity Fair* appeared with its famous Spy cartoons, and *Lippincott's Monthly Magazine* serialized Oscar Wilde's *Picture of Dorian Gray* and Conan Doyle's *Sign of Four*. Magazines were political, satirical or merely entertaining, and the competition for the male reader was intense. We lack accurate data on readership, profiles and circulation in the Victorian period, so it would be unwise to assume that these magazines were read only or even principally by men, but a look at the advertising they carried rather support that impression. Motor cars were beginning to replace the horse and carriage, and they were deemed to be a male interest. Tobacco advertising had begun to appear. W.D. & H.O. Wills, promoting their Capstan Navy Cut tobacco, pictured two gold miners under the headline 'The Only Comfort in Klondyke'. A grizzled old miner is extending his hand with the caption 'See those nuggets? I'd give the lot for another tin of Will's Capstans.' The much-advertised safety razor had arrived from America, although the cut-throat was still the clean-shaven gentleman's shaving tool of choice.

The press was booming. As the egalitarian Clarence Moran wrote in 1905, 'Every rank of society, from the highest to the lowest, reads newspapers. For those who cannot aspire to *The Times*, or even the penny dailies, a multitude of half-penny journals is published every morning and evening. There is, in fact, no class of consumers who cannot be reached through the medium of some section or other of the press.' This universality may have contributed to the decline of the men's magazine by the time of the First World War, allowing, of course, for the huge shift of manpower to the Western Front. The exception was the *Gentleman's Pall Mall*, which first appeared, rather inopportunely, in 1914 and concentrated almost entirely on fashion for gentlemen.

Men's magazines were thereafter pretty rare until 1935, when Pearsons (later Newnes) published the first issue of its trend-setting pocket magazine *Men Only*. This was unequivocally a man's title. The opening editorial stated:

> This is a magazine for men only. Until today, every magazine
> published in this country has been produced with at least one eye
> on the woman reader. We don't want women readers. We won't
> have women readers. Will men buy a magazine with a hundred
> per cent masculine appeal? Of course they will. Haven't you stood

at a railway bookstall and watched the poor fellows searching for something that wasn't an insult to their intelligence? Haven't you seen them turn sadly away from all that castrated nonsense and go to sleep in a corner of the carriage for want of something better to do?

The magazine lived up to its title. The editorial reeked of tobacco smoke, sweaty sports, misogyny, chauvinism, xenophobia, homophobia, rugger buggers and racism. The advertising it carried followed suit, focusing on shaving, drink, clothes and golf balls (although Spalding upset the apple cart by suggesting that their balls were not 'for men only but women too'). Rupture appliances and self-help books were also frequently advertised.

Men Only was an instant bookstall success. The Editor positively hugged himself with self-congratulation in the second issue: 'Candour compels us to admit that *Men Only* was an overwhelming success from the word go.' The pocket-size formula was also popular. The editorial in the second issue was, if anything, even more male-oriented. 'No more women in the office, Thank you!' 'Marriage is carrying love too far.' Sometimes the mood turned serious and a bit nasty:

Nearly every man loves some one woman. For whom he is willing to work and sacrifice, yet he may have an inarticulate grudge against women as a sex. Prick him with a threat to his job, put the responsibility of an extra or an unloved woman upon him, and it will break out. Men are critical of a sex which has become competitive and expensive; whose financial and industrial achievements are taking bread out of men's mouths; whose mortality has become erratic, undisciplined, and unreliable and yet claim the protection of the law; and whose social cost is no longer justified by their domestic industry nor by the extent of their child-bearing.

The Second World War gave a huge circulation boost to *Men Only*, together with similar titles. Because of paper rationing, the pocket size had shrunk even smaller, but it was hugely popular with the Forces. Each issue carried a ration of one naked lady, designated by her Christian name (Doreen, Verity or whatever), and only a tantalizing glimpse of a single nipple was vouchsafed. Gone was the overt misogyny. But by the end of the war the magazine looked tired.

The publisher, Newnes, also owned *London Opinion*, a humorous pocket magazine whose cover always featured a puppet figure of an old colonel with a large bushy moustache. The magazine carried a monthly feature about a girl called Myrtle, an ingenuous virgin who was always getting into ribald and complicated situations. But circulation was fading, and Newnes closed the title. It disappeared into *Men Only*, which plodded on, full of rather crass cartoons (desert islands, cannibals, women drivers, dumb chorus girls and so on). There was no nakedness but coloured plates of 'cheesecake' with long-legged young women in bathing dress. It carried plenty of one-liners, but the tone was considerably milder than before. Readers complained that the magazine now lacked the old locker-room humour. The magazine had lost its way, and Newnes decided to sell it to the Soho entrepreneur Paul Raymond, who turned it into a 'skin' magazine.

The pocket-magazine concept was popular before and during the war. Publishers liked it because it used less paper. Two years after *Men Only* came *Lilliput* from Hulton Press. The title, of course, was perfect for a small format. The magazine cost only 6d, just half the cover price of *Men Only*, and featured a hundred pages of articles, stories and cartoons. It became famous for its photographic jokes, which juxtaposed two contrasting pictures with witty linking captions. The idea for the magazine came from Stephen Lorant, a Hungarian refugee from Nazi Germany where he had built a reputation as a journalist and editor. He set up Pocket Publications to launch *Lilliput*, but Edward Hulton was convinced that Lorant was the man to edit his new *Picture Post*, so he bought out Lorant and *Lilliput* became a Hulton magazine. Lorant edited both publications, the photo weekly during the week and the small monthly at weekends. But he left England in 1940 for America, frustrated that the authorities were treating him as an enemy alien. The new Editor appointed to run both magazines was Tom Hopkinson, a job he occupied throughout the war.

The editorial emphasis was on humour. The Assistant Editor was Kaye Webb, later to marry one of the magazine's most frequent cartoonists, Ronald Searle. As with all the wartime magazines, demand from the travelling public and the Forces was constant, and every copy was sold out. Although the magazine was originally aimed at both sexes, it increasingly became a men's magazine, particularly in the minds of the advertisement department (of which I was a member in the 1950s). It remained a creative magazine, however, full of fun and good writing. The nudes were always tasteful, and it carried articles by Hemingway, Betjeman, Osbert Sitwell and Bernard Shaw. A regular contributor after the war was Patrick Campbell, who became a staff member. Its end came swiftly after Hulton Press was sold to Odhams in 1959, and the new owners closed it shortly afterwards.

These little magazines shared a common factor: they all had a sense of humour, which has so often been lacking in later magazines for men.

A magazine which had little time for humour was an eccentric but popular title that Newnes had launched back in 1898. *Wide World* was a curiosity, a *Boy's Own* paper for grown-up men or at least for those who hankered after a life of adventure and thrills, even if they were sitting on the 8.15 from Basingstoke or in the comfort of a suburban armchair. The magazine cost 1s. 6d. monthly, and the editorial was packed with testosterone. The front cover declared itself 'The Magazine for Men'. Its unique selling point was true-life adventure, and every contribution, the Editor warned, 'had to be strictly original and true in every detail'. Many stories were accompanied by reproductions of newspaper cuttings as proof that they were true. And what stories! The magazine bulged with tales of gold mining, treasure hunts, haunted ships, voodoo, bank robberies, black magic, man-eating sharks, big-game hunting, grizzly bears and other macho adventures. Quintessential to many of the stories was the image of the white man as a demi-god to simple, superstitious natives. The white man was a model of responsibility, courage and authority. Johnnie Foreigners were given little truck. Each issue also carried a section called 'Man and His Needs. A Monthly Causerie of Matters Masculine', written by 'The Captain', a stickler for the right attire and correct male grooming. His columns reflect a strongly misogynistic bent. *Wide World* met its end in the late 1950s, its demise perhaps hastened by the arrival of commercial television.

Two other titles, very popular with servicemen but surviving the war, were *Razzle* and *Blighty*, weeklies displaying innate vulgarity and man appeal. The latter was generous enough to carry an occasional humorous column from me when I served on a Forces radio station in 1946 in Vienna. They dished out a beneficent £2 for my contributions. Both these cheap and unsubtle weeklies passed away in the 1950s.

Upmarket men's magazines began to emerge a decade later. John Taylor, the Editor of *Tailor and Cutter*, brought out a pocket-sized quarterly, *Man about Town*, largely devoted to fashion but with some humorous lifestyle features. It was later acquired by Haymarket Press and edited by Nicholas Tomalin. They changed to the title to *About Town* and later simply *Town*. It became a smart, sophisticated monthly, endeavouring to compete with *Queen* for the attention of 1960s' style set but still maintaining a strong masculine appeal. Some competition came from the USA with an attempt to bring out a British edition of *Esquire*, but that soon failed. The actor and director Bryan Forbes fancied a stab at the market with *King*, an obvious effort to compete against *Queen*, but that also staggered to an early death.

The next phase in the story of the male press came with the 'skin' mags. The genesis was the famous American *Playboy*, with its glamorous centrefolds of ladies in the discreet altogether. Britain followed with Bob Guccione's *Penthouse*, which kicked the market along by showing pubic hair, eschewing the censorious airbrush. 'Swinging Britain' was the perfect medium for the rapid growth of erotic voyeur magazines, resulting in the introduction of the 'top shelf', a device to put offending magazines out of the reach of curious children in the newsagents'.

Over time the photographs became more gynaecological as new titles poured into the 'adult' magazine sector, welcomed by small backstreet newsagents and motorway shops. One would like to think that all this smutty publishing would run its course, but after fifty years many magazines of that type are still on the top shelf, offering an endless parade of mammaries and pudenda. The major publishers resisted the temptation to join the parade, although IPC launched *Club*, aimed directly at the new young audience which found *Playboy* and *Penthouse* so irresistible, but there were no nudes. *Club* soon closed for lack of circulation, to the amusement of the more realistic purveyors of the semi-pornographic.

Things began to change when more sophisticated titles came on the scene. Fashion was their principal component, together with an inclination towards the trendy. Nick Logan's company Wagadon was the pioneer, closely watched by the big publishers when it launched *The Face*, which promised 'Everything new, exciting and likely to appear everywhere else twelve months later'. The newcomer was a success, and twelve months later Wagadon followed with *Arena*, aimed at 18–35-year-old men, with a strong emphasis on fashion but occasional forays into the more sexual side of men's lives. One issue printed pictures of Naomi Campbell's breasts over six pages. Condé Nast ventured into the new market with a British version of *GQ*. *GQ* was doing well in the USA after an inconsistent history: it had begun life as *Apparel Arts* as a pre-war trade magazine and was then relaunched as *Gentlemen's Quarterly*. Despite the name, the present magazine is a monthly, but then in Australia *Woman's Weekly* is a quarterly.

Hard on the heels of *GQ* came the British edition of *Esquire*, an American title famous for its 'good writing' before the war. The new import was plagued with launch problems, and editors briskly followed one another through the revolving doors of National Magazines House. Eventually Rosie Boycott, a woman of considerable editorial talent, was taken on, and the magazine began to achieve more stable success.

'Before we came along, men's magazines were constipated.' So said James Brown, the Editor of *Loaded*, a title surprisingly and uncharacteristically launched by IPC in 1994. *Loaded* exploded on to the market like thousands of cans of lager released at a football match on a Saturday afternoon. It came out fighting, happy to break all the rules and totally uninterested in the type of buttoned-down readers being sought by the stylish glossies. The cover line defined the editorial ethos: 'For Men Who Should Know Better'. Their reader was the 'new bloke': his interests were footie, drinking, comedy clubs, clobber and getting his leg over. *Loaded* was fruity, cocksure, adolescent, scatological and irreverent and completely in sync with the permissive, anarchic lifestyle of thousands of young men with disposable incomes and free-and-easy sex lives. Its circulation soared, and nothing seemed barred. Even the film reviews carried words that one was unlikely to hear in a tea shop in the Cotswolds over scones and fairy cakes.

One can imagine the inhabitants of the IPC boardroom being uncomfortably surprised by their new best-seller, rather like a respectable city clerk discovering his wife is on the game, making lots of money, but don't tell the neighbours. It was all a long way from the prissy, lukewarm *Club*.

Loaded was a true original in British publishing, a bold idea energized by a team of iconoclastic young journalists given the luxury of a free rein. Its success is a tribute to IPC's courage in recognizing that the product could fit the market and going for it. The final product was a bit like the Marx Brothers at the Raymond Revue Bar via *Viz*, but no one can deny that *Loaded* caught the *Zeitgeist*.

EMAP had purchased a mild magazine called *For Him Magazine* which mutated it into *FHM*. The revitalized product, backed by EMAP financial resources, went straight for the population of sexually aware young men with a heady mixture of provocative features, health problems and all the earthy delights of being young and priapic with a bit of spare cash. Circulation soared, and *FHM* soon became the market leader in a sector which was buoyantly breaking sales records.

Felix Dennis could not stand by and miss out on this profitable new market, and he brought out *Maxim* in 1995 with a handsome budget and a blues cassette as a cover-mount. His star editor was Gill Hudson, at the helm of *Company*, who set out to make the new title a sort of male *Cosmopolitan*. Sex permeated the pages, but the magazine was always literate, ballsy, factual and fun. Hudson left after establishing a successful title and took over the editorship of the *Radio Times*.

If men always have sex on their minds, male health seems to run it a close second. The first magazine to concentrate on the subject was *XL*, and later entrants were *Men's Health* and *Men's Fitness*.

The men's sector took a tumble as the 2000s arrived. There were some uncomfortable losses, but by the middle of 2008 *FHM* was recording 280,000 and *Loaded* puffing along behind with 95,000. The eight monthly titles combined still reach a monthly sale of 1 million copies.

Successes can sometimes be counterbalanced by failures. I confess that in 1978 I thought I had a clever idea when I suggested a male version of *Cosmopolitan*. *Cosmopolitan Man* was produced for only one issue, with a sell-out print order of 150,000 and carrying sixty pages of male-relevant advertising. However, the production value was poor and much of the editorial on the plodding side. Advertisers were very keen to see such a title succeed, and I planned to move the magazine to our German printers and raise the print order to 400,000. This was a financial gamble at a time when conditions were poor, and my masters in New York felt that we should not proceed. It was a disappointment, but we lacked the publishing courage to back it and turn it into at least a quarterly and later a monthly. It was therefore particularly galling when we later saw the massive success of magazines in the category. The subsequent American go-ahead for us to publish *Esquire* was no consolation. In my view, *Cosmopolitan Man* could have turned out to be a 'gusher'.

A publishing dream, a mythical Elysium, for publishers working in the male market was a weekly magazine for men – not one in the *Razzle* category but a weekly with general features that would be of sufficient interest to men to purchase the title fifty-two times a year. Of course, the newspapers, which always have a strong male readership (for the sport?), have taken to running supplements and features for men covering their health and grooming interests. But despite the success of titles for 'the lads' and the newer glossy monthlies, there was still no sign at the turn of the century of a weekly for men appearing on the bookstalls.

Suddenly, like the famous Number 11 bus, there came not one weekly but two! This was an exciting prospect. Further good news was that they were being published by two of the most illustrious magazine publishers in the country, IPC and EMAP, rather than some sordid back-street publisher who would inevitably cater for the prurient and voyeuristic. The first splash of cold water, however, came with the advance publicity. The title of the IPC contribution to male edification was to be *Nuts*. Was this an oblique reference to the male sexual apparatus? Would the publisher have preferred the title *Bollocks* if they had been bold enough? Or did it refer to insanity in the editorial offices, some kind of Marx Brothers high jinks to amuse us with its crackpot humour and jokey topicality? Very confusing.

Then came the contribution from EMAP. This, enigmatically, was to be entitled *Zoo*. Surely this would confuse naturalists? I seem to remember back in the hazy days of my boyhood in the 1940s, when I showed an interest in such matters, that there was a magazine called *Zoo* which I bought occasionally with my pocket money. Or did the title imply in some Freudian way that life was like a zoo and men were simply animals? It could of course also refer to a noisy group of young people, apposite to the binge-drinking crowd.

What a disappointment the new magazines were when they arrived – pages and pages of tits, footie, vulgar letters, minimal 'fashion', rude joke pages and, of course, television listings. They were not quite Neanderthal, but you could hear knuckles scraping along the ground. They both retail at £1.60 each, carry 108 pages and are practically mirror reflections of each other, often using identical ideas for features. *Nuts* is perhaps more sexually upfront. In the issue I dissected, the naked-tit count was an eye-glazing forty-four, while *Zoo* restrained itself at a mere dozen. *Nuts* liked the bosoms bare, while *Zoo* stuffed them into bras and bikini tops. The jokes in *Nuts* were basic and often crude, while its competitor's were much more modest.

Football was of course an important ingredient in both, one carrying seven pages on the subject and the other nine. *Nuts* carried fourteen pages of detailed TV, while *Zoo's* 'readers' were given only highlights. When either publication carried a newsy feature, it told the story in pictures with minimal text. The advertising content was fairly similar in both magazines, *Nuts* with fourteen pages of display and five pages of unsubtle text dating and sex videos, while *Zoo* had eleven display pages but seven pages of sex advertising with some very explicit invitations. The circulation of *Zoo* at the end of 2007 stood at 179,000 (a drop of 12.5 per cent from the previous year), and *Nuts* was winning the circulation battle at 270,000 (a fall of 8.5 per cent). By mid-summer 2008 *Zoo* had dropped to 161,000 and *Nuts* to 250,000.

I will be considered by some to be a wet blanket, criticizing these icons of youthful society. If the publishers have found a market, then they are running successful businesses. However, I must deplore the low standards considered necessary to engage the minds of their readerships. Surely at least one of the publishing duo could have developed a new formula, aiming higher than the Y-fronts. But each week they pump out 216 pages of paper imitating each other's editorial grot with material that is unflattering to the intellect of the male sex. The men's market is still at a wobbly stage.

5

THE 1990S

NEWSPAPER TYCOONS MAKE THEIR OWN NEWS,
ONE WITH A SPLASH

–

RICHARD DESMOND BUYS THE *DAILY EXPRESS*

–

METRO, THE FIRST GIVE-AWAY, APPEARS

–

MAGAZINES ARE LAUNCHED IN RECORD NUMBERS,
AND THERE ARE RECORD CLOSURES

–

TIME WARNER BUYS IPC, AND BIG IS BEAUTIFUL

The 1990s began with an explosive headline story about the media. Robert Maxwell, the highly controversial publisher and owner of the Mirror Group, had disappeared overboard from his yacht *Lady Ghislaine* in the Mediterranean. Rumours immediately began to fly around the business world. Was he pushed? Was it suicide? There were stories of complicated contracts with Israeli Intelligence, possible bankruptcy, a drunken slip off the deck – the mystery fascinated the world's press. The theories ranged from the possible, through the probable, to the highly unlikely. Murderous stowaways were mentioned and hitmen hired by rival publishers. It was later revealed that he had been financing some of his arcane deals with the Mirror Pension Fund, which suggested that he killed himself to escape an impending scandal.

The Maxwell story is intriguing. The son of a Czech peasant, he had served as an officer in the Queen's Royal Regiment during the invasion of Europe, winning the Military Cross, which he received from General Montgomery. He entered the publishing scene with Pergamon Press in Oxford, publishing scientific papers from Eastern Europe. When I worked at *New Scientist*, which advertised his journals, he was always happy to see us at his grand headquarters at Headington Hall near Oxford.

His early attempts to buy a national newspaper were frustrated. He became involved in 1974 with the *Scottish Daily News*, a venture that lasted only six months. But he became Chairman of the British Printing Corporation, later renamed the Maxwell Communication Corporation; he saved BPC from bankruptcy and became a hero in the City. In 1984 he bought the Mirror Group from Reed International for £113 million. His attempt to launch a London evening newspaper came to an expensive failure when he was outmanoeuvred by Rothermere. Always looking to create a sensation, he offered a bingo prize of £1 million, a jackpot never seen before. He appeared on television: 'I'm waiting to make you a millionaire.' But he was scooped by the *Sun* which offered the same prize and revealed their winner before the *Daily Mirror* could find theirs.

His relations with the print unions at the *Mirror* were tempestuous. After many tactical manoeuvres he scored a victory over the unions and brought an end to the historic overmanning at the paper, which included Fleet Street 'Spanish practices' and other excesses. Altogether 2,100 employees were made redundant, and their payouts were funded from the Mirror Pension Fund. Annual savings, as a consequence, were over £40 million.

Maxwell was a supreme personal promoter and a born fighter. He continued to battle with the unions, his publishing rivals and his staff right up to his mysterious death. His financial shenanigans must have been labyrinthine and secret to many around him.

Just before he purchased the *Daily Mirror*, at a time when his activities in the printing business were controversial, I organized a lunch for four hundred newspaper, magazine and printing executives at the Royal Lancaster Hotel with Maxwell as guest of honour and speaker. I was warned by many people that he was notorious for not turning up at such events. I safeguarded against that embarrassment by careful liaison with his second-in-command, and to my relief my guest of honour duly appeared on time. He performed splendidly. He made an incisive speech, facing up to a critical crowd. He even, ironically, indulged in a ding-dong argument across the floor with executives on the *Daily Mirror* table. He even offered my son, a guest at the top table who had just completed a course at the London College of Printing, a job which he honoured next morning. He was a rogue but not the first such to stride across the Fleet Street stage – and probably not the last.

Another magnetic proprietor took to the Fleet Street stage at the end of the century. Richard Desmond, long active in the world of top-shelf magazines and saucy television channels, emulated the outstanding success of *Hello!* by introducing a rival celebrity magazine, *OK!*, in 1993. The editorial formula was identical to the Spanish original, and the new entrant was willing to pay large sums of money for exclusive wedding pictures of the famous. *OK!*'s circulation soared to 600,000 by 2008, seventh in the circulation list of the top fifty consumer magazines, leaving *Hello!* way down the circulation table with 280,000.

Desmond bought the *Daily Express* in 2000 for a bargain price of £25 million which included the *Sunday Express*. With these two properties he moved into middle-market competition with the *Daily Mail* and the *Mail on Sunday*, but he still has a formidable mountain to climb to top the Rothermere papers. He rid himself of his top-shelf magazines, probably under the impression that *Asian Babes* sat uncomfortably with his new and more prestigious acquisitions. In 2005 he moved the *Express* from its Blackfriars Bridge headquarters across the river to Upper Thames Street.

The rest of the popular press – and *Private Eye* – is fascinated by the doings of the new Fleet Street tycoon, particularly with the money he awards himself. *The Times* city diary noted in May 2008 that, apart from putting £40 million into the *Express* Pension Fund, Desmond had purchased a £17 million Gulfstream. It pointed out that the last Fleet Street media owner to buy a corporate jet was Lord Black, but it added that at least Desmond could afford it and had the free time to use it!

A trail-blazing event in 1999, which is having considerable consequences in the 2000s, was the launch of Associated Newspaper's *Metro*, a morning newspaper given away free at railway and tube stations to people who don't generally read newspapers. Associated then followed with a free lunchtime version of the *Evening Standard* called *Lite*, which it was. Murdoch's counter-attack was to produce the *London Paper*, which is given away free by an army of distributors. Later *Lite* was also given away in the evening rush hour. Newsprint manufacturers are delighted, London Underground station cleaners less so.

In 1994 the Mirror Group, reeling from the Maxwell débâcle, acquired Midland Independent Newspapers, which included the *Birmingham Post and Mail.* They also acquired the licence to publish the *Racing Post*. Then they joined the Fleet Street exodus when they moved out of their impressive building dominating Holborn Circus and settled in Canary Wharf. In 1999 the Mirror Group merged with Trinity plc to create Trinity Mirror, in the process having to sell the *Belfast Telegraph* to the Independent News and Media company. Later in the year they added eighty titles to their regional portfolio with the acquisition of Southnews. Trinity Mirror was now Britain's largest newspaper publisher, with over 250 titles.

The magazine business was still in start-and-stop mode in the 1990s. The 'hatches and dispatches' list was as bloody as the 1980s: out of twenty-six starts, fifteen died in the same decade, many quite quickly. But it was also a lethal period for many older titles. IPC closed a crop of titles including *Living*, *Homes and Ideas*, *Options*, *Nova* (second time around), *Woman's Journal* and *19*. Other departures included *Punch* (the Harrods version), *Spare Rib* and the adolescent *Jackie*.

Title	Owner	Launched	Died
BBC Family Life	BBC	1998	1998
BBC Good Health	BBC	1992	1993
BBC Vegetarian Food	BBC	1997	1998
Beautiful Homes	IPC	1998	
Condé Nast Traveller	Condé Nast	1997	
Eat Soup!	IPC	1996	1997
Enjoy!	Bauer	1996	1997
Eva	IPC	1994	1998
Frank	Wagadon	1997	1999
Film and TV Weekly	IPC	1996	1996
Guess Who?	Harmsworth	1993	1993
Here	Gruner and Jahr	1996	1997
Homes and Antiques	BBC	1993	
Let's Cook!	Bauer	1990	1991
M	National Magazines	1990	1991
Maxim	Dennis	1995	
Metropolitan Home	Harmsworth	1990	1990

Title	Owner	Launched	Died
Mirabella	Murdoch	1990	1991
Puzzle Week	IPC	1992	1993
Red	EMAP	1998	
Shout	D.C. Thomson	1991	
Take a Break	Bauer	1990	
That's Life	Bauer	1995	
Top Santé	EMAP	1993	
Waitrose Food	John Brown	1999	
Zest	National Magazines	1996	

IPC attempted to revive the ailing *Woman's Realm* in 1998 with a new logo and cover design, concentrating on women in the over-45 age bracket. The announced target was 'empty nesters', and the Editor Kathy Weston told the trade press: 'The magazine will concentrate less about getting a child to sleep and more on women who are experiencing a new start after the children have left home.' But not only had the children left, so had the readers, and the magazine was closed in 2001, merged into another tottering veteran, *Woman's Weekly*.

In 1998 National Magazines ventured into the burgeoning parenting market when they launched *M*. I thought the title itself was curiously inapt. I advised the managing director, Terry Mansfield, that *M* was the name of the classic Fritz Lang thriller starring Peter Lorre in which he played a sinister child murderer. Surely this was an inappropriate title for a magazine aimed at mothers with young children. In any event the magazine was closed the following year, probably strangled in a dark alley.

Now for a *rara avis*: a home-grown publisher of women's magazines. The BBC had moved into magazines with titles closely allied to their television programmes, but rival commercial publishers had objected when they strayed outside these limits. They need not have worried unduly. *BBC Family Life* lasted only eight months. As a BBC director said: 'Although we had a positive feedback from our pre-launch research, this didn't translate into the expected level of sales. *BBC Family Life* is an excellent magazine for its target market and readers have been very appreciative, but there simply aren't enough people prepared to buy it on a regular basis.' *BBC Good Health* was launched in 1992 but staggered on only until the following year. Another BBC failure was the *Clothes Show* magazine, which had been linked for several years with a successful road show. Nor did *BBC Vegetarian Food*, launched in 1992, last as long as it takes a carrot to grow.

A big flop in 1997 was *Film and TV Week*, which IPC targeted at the prosperous television listings market. They aimed for a modest 150,000 circulation, but inside sources lamented that actual sales were about 50,000. The title was closed after two months. The management seemed rather hurt and claimed that advertising was 'roughly on target', although the last issue contained only a page advertisement for Maltesers and a house advertisement for another IPC title. The managing director, Nigel Davidson, said: 'We will be doing a lot of work to find out why it didn't sell. We never made a secret of the fact that we knew this was going to be difficult.' The words 'stable' and 'door' spring to mind.

The television listings market had been 'deregulated' in 1990, creating a publishing free-for-all. Anybody could publish a listings magazine, providing they paid royalties to the BBC or ITV. Until then only the *Radio Times* could carry details of BBC programmes and *TV Times* monopolized the commercial stations. Following deregulation there were several starts and stops. By 2008 there were ten titles jostling for a place in the market against the classic *Radio Times*. Bauer had three: *TV Choice*, *TV Quick* and *Total TV Guide*. IPC published four: *What's on TV*, *TV Times*, *TV Easy* and

TV and Satellite Week, plus the niche *Soaplife*. Hachette Filipacchi also owned a sudsy title with *Inside Soap*. Together they were achieving a circulation of almost 5 million copies every week, which is remarkable when all the daily and evening papers carry very detailed listings, and all the celeb titles also have a listings section.

During the 1990s several newspaper publishers ventured into the magazine minefield without success. Harmsworth, publishers of the *Daily Mail*, decided to enter the escalating homes magazine area, cutting a deal with the American company Meredith. of the new magazine was called *Metropolitan Home*, and the editorial ethos, according to the Editor Dee Nolan, was 'to bring a fresh editorial approach to what has been traditionally a decorating or nostalgia-led home interest coverage. Our reports will cover what's new, what's good, what's amusing in the areas of design, food, restaurants, transport, gardening, architecture, interiors, travel.' Advertisers were irritatingly reluctant to spend in the title, and it closed within the year. Harmsworth also ventured into the puzzle market, another field that seemed to have endless possibilities, although in the UK it was dominated by the Dutch publisher VNU. They had a go with *Guess Who?* in 1993, but this also bit the dust within the same year.

Rupert Murdoch, having dipped his toe into the women's market pond with the import *New Woman*, went further in 1990 with the domestic launch of another American title, *Mirabella*, a monthly glossy with a high cover price. It ran for only nine issues under the editorship of Lesley White. Sales were reputed to be only 50,000, presenting no potential threat to the established glossies. Dismissing trade criticism, White said that 'although two hundred pages are born of a commercial venture, they are also, above all else, an overriding, fingers crossed act of faith'. Fingers uncrossed, Murdoch sold the magazine company to EMAP and concentrated on the national press.

The gloom and doom hanging over the magazines sector continued. In 1999 IPC closed *Options*, launched back in 1982 as 'The way you want to live now'. It was successful in the mid-market, with a good reputation for fashion, but sales slid to 119,000, and, after one of those 'relaunches' on which the magazine business always pins such faith, the decision was to close it. Perhaps this was not unconnected with the announcement from IPC in the same week that they were making two hundred redundancies across the company. The *Evening Standard*, in a slight gloat, reported that the 'circulation had dropped steadily during the 1990s – clearly and reassuringly, a decade in need of more pressing information than where to buy that next little black number'.

EMAP closed their teenage magazine *Big!* after a ten-year publishing span which saw a 41 per cent drop in sales. An EMAP executive eloquently observed: 'We have not seen a sufficient sustainable uplift in trading.'

Another IPC casualty in the 1990s was *Eva*, a weekly which pussyfooted around the *Cosmopolitan* formula with eye-catching cover lines – eye-catching, that is, to the more prurient who found the traditional weeklies too mumsy. Its strapline 'For the girl who wants it all' was strongly reminiscent of Helen Gurley Brown's famous slogan 'Having it all', and it suffered a 30 per cent drop in sales in three years. The news trade magazine *Retail Newsagent* reported that the women's weekly market accounted for 30 per cent of all consumer magazines sold in the country but that the sector was under fierce pressure, some analysts rather mysteriously blaming the national lottery. *Eva* was given the chop in the same week that the BBC closed *Tomorrow's World*, a failure in a niche market.

Bauer was also having troubles and closed *Let's Cook!* and *Enjoy!* Maybe it was those irritating exclamation marks! However, they discovered a new niche in the weekly market: the coffee break. They brought out *Take a Break*, aimed at the busy housewife stopping for a cup of instant at eleven o'clock and picking up the magazine whose editorial content would not overstretch their busy minds. The innovation met with instant success, and eighteen years later *Take a Break* sits at the top of the consumer magazine table (below the listings titles) with a circulation not far off 1 million. That almost equals the sales of *Woman's Own*, *Woman* and *Woman's Weekly* combined. Five years later Bauer launched the similar *That's Life*, which currently sells over 450,000.

An old canard in the newspaper business is that the dream of many Fleet Street hacks is to retire from the hurly-burly of the newsroom and the unpleasantness of grouchy news editors and start their own magazine. It all starts with an idea, probably originating in a beery chat in the local after a hard day's work or perhaps there is sudden inspiration in the bath with the thought that 'nobody's done a magazine on celebrity cats' or whatever. I make no suggestion that Eve Pollard, after a distinguished career as Editor of the *Daily Express* and the *Sunday Pictorial*, ever participated in beery sessions, although she probably did take a bath at times, but her lightbulb moment encouraged her to launch *Wedding Day* in 1999. There is now a lively market in weddings, as huge sums are spent on weddings and, of course, *the dress*. There was nothing wrong with Pollard's concept or the editorial execution, but the market was well covered with competitors, and new launches need ongoing financial backing. Pollard's company, Parkhill, also launched *Aura*, aimed at the thirty-plus woman and had plans for a celebrity magazine. However, it all went sour, and Pollard had to confess to the trade press: 'We have two good magazines that readers like, but we needed more backing to publish additional magazines, and for sales promotion, and could not find it in time. The barriers to entry for small independent publishers of upmarket, glossy magazines are formidable.' Her words ring true. The world of women's magazines is not for under-financed minnows.

Parenting and puzzles appear to be magazine subjects that attract failures, notwithstanding a few successes over the years. EMAP gave up publishing *Parents*, excusing themselves with the rationale that the market for parents with older children was not viable and the need was for magazines focusing on pregnancy, birth and babies' first year. Puzzles proved to be an enigma for IPC: their well-promoted *Puzzles Weekly* tried to break into a very crowded market and was abandoned within the year.

In 1997 another brainwave suggested to a company called XL Communications that your friendly milkman could drop off a magazine with your daily pinta. Maggie Goodman, launch Editor of *Company* and *Hello!*, was recruited as Editor of *Home and Life* with a circulation target of 300,000. But like so many bright ideas before it, the title failed to deliver.

Even Homer nods. Gruner and Jahr decided to join the gossipy celebrity flood by launching *Here!* in 1996, but it was soon sold to IPC, who tucked it into its like-minded organ, *Now*.

IPC decided in 1996 to move into the food-and-drink sector. They gave their entrant the wacky title *Eat Soup*, entrusting it to the editorial team who ran the highly successful men's magazine *Loaded*. The editorial content was straightforward: food, drink and travel aimed at the readership of the *Loaded* brand. Perhaps an eccentric title merely confuses, or else the editorial did not connect with its target, and the magazine closed the following year.

A publication that had enjoyed a rather longer lifespan was the classic *Punch*, launched in 1814. It suffered in later years from the old chestnut that 'it's not as funny as it used to be'. During and after the Second World War, under the editorships of Malcolm Muggeridge, Basil Boothroyd and Alan Coren, the magazine became a witty and trendy commentary on the British way of life. But by the 1970s it seemed to run out of steam, failing to appeal to a younger audience, and it closed down. Rather surprisingly, in 1996 the title was resurrected by Mohamed Al-Fayed, the owner of Harrods, not renowned for his publishing expertise or his appreciation of British wit. He launched the title as a weekly but soon reverted to fortnightly publishing. Research told him that 'many readers who buy the magazine do not necessarily take every issue because of their high reading load', a sentiment echoed by the publishers of *Private Eye*, who have always been firm adherents of fortnightly publication. But even the reduction in frequency failed to work for *Punch* and Al-Fayed threw in the towel in 2002.

The year 1995 saw the throttling of *Living* by IPC. This was the supermarkets-only magazine originated by Roy Thomson in 1967 to join his *Family Circle*. The two titles had been sold on to IPC, but their days were numbered as the supermarkets were now flooded with magazines covering the same domestic subjects and mostly with better editorial. The following year *Family Circle* was treated to a new design and the boost of a £2.5 million publicity budget; now it was not to be sold in supermarkets but only through conventional news-trade outlets. The ploy failed, and the old title was put out of its misery in 2006. It had served its progenitor profitably in its time.

There were some successes. Condé Nast decided to publish their successful American title *Condé Nast Traveler* in the UK, adding an 'l' to the masthead. Despite the clumsy name, the title was a hit with its enviable descriptions of spas and exotic watering holes for the affluent. Of course mere mortals can only dream, but there is certainly a market for vicarious travel luxury, just as the fashion glossies are bursting with advertisements for astronomically priced fashion accessories and jewellery. The holiday market has often been an elephant's graveyard for magazines over the years, but under the editorship of Sarah Miller Condé Nast got this one right.

Other 1990s hits include *Zest* from National Magazines and *Top*

Santé from Hachette – two bright monthlies exploiting our desire to be thin and healthy.

Names have often been the strength and sometimes the weakness of new magazines. In the capacious world of women's magazines it is now quite contrary to put the word 'woman' in the title. Publishers look on the word as very 1930s, with connotations of the housewife and the little woman, so they bend over backwards to create new titles which sound modish and eye-catching. This must have been a problem for EMAP when they were seeking a title for their new fashion and feature magazine in 1998. The managing director of EMAP tells the story that he went out alone for dinner when the new magazine was on the drawing-board to concentrate on finding a suitable title. He glanced at the bottle of claret on his table and the word 'red' flashed into his mind. So out came a glossy publication aimed at the thirtysomething market, backed by a strong campaign and achieving 180,000 sales. The head of marketing at EMAP Elan, Anne-Marie Lavan, said that the success of the title was its capture of the 'middle youth' market, perhaps a convoluted way of saying mid-thirties.

A competitor to *Red* appeared from the BBC in 2000. This was the Beeb's first venture into the fashionable women's feature market, and they launched a first-class glossy magazine called *Eve*. EMAP saw the newcomer as a direct threat to *Red*, which they backed with a £1 million campaign on the day the BBC title was launched. Strangely, both the magazines had new owners within five years. *Red* moved to Hachette after a buy-out, and the BBC was forced to sell *Eve* because the subject was not deemed to have a BBC connection. Michael Heseltine's Haymarket Publishing were quick to seize *Eve*, and they have successfully developed it.

John Brown, the original publisher in Newcastle of the sophisticated comic *Viz*, which featured the The Fat Slags and Johnny Fartpants among others, sold the title to concentrate on contract publishing. This new form of magazine enterprise had been considerably lifted with the success of *M&S Magazine* for Marks and Spencer, published by Redwood. Suddenly everybody seemed to want to publish magazines for their brand – estate agents and stores leading the way. The supermarkets were particularly eager, and their offerings were mostly given away in store. The exception was Sainsbury's, who sold their title to their customers. John Brown had already launched *Food Illustrated* as a paid-for glossy gourmet title but was approached by Waitrose to develop their in-store magazine, which would be sold at the checkout. He closed his own title to initiate the supermarket title. At the same time he decided to move into the glossy fashion market by launching the curiously named *Bare*. He was aware that Condé Nast were about to launch *Glamour* and also that Bauer had intentions in the same market. In cavalier tone, Brown told *Media Week* that 'I may be a fool not to be concerned, but firstly we can't do anything about it, so why waste time worrying. Our competitors in the market are bloody great companies that need bloody great profit margins and they put lots of money into their magazines. That's not our way.' But with modest circulation aims of only 50,000, Brown found this was a different game to contract publishing, and his magazine left the world in the following year.

Approaching the millennium, as the internet prepared to sweep all before it and technological innovations arrived at an ever-accelerating pace, the print media were clearly going to find the going tough. But they were not about to fade away either. We still had eleven national daily newspapers, eleven national Sundays and a strong regional press. The magazine business, which had been through a couple of cathartic decades, still had the energy and inventiveness to reinvent itself.

Following the turbulence of the previous thirty years, ownership of the major newspaper titles seemed to settle down. As the decade drew to a close, Richard Desmond with his *Daily Express* squared up to Rothermere, Murdoch, Trinity Mirror and the Barclay Twins, the reclusive new proprietors of the Telegraph Group. A new battle was now engaged for circulation and profit in the context of a declining readership and the new propensity to give away newspapers free.

The magazine business experienced two major changes of ownership at this time. Gruner and Jahr, the original German invaders of the British women's magazine market in 1986, were finding the competition too hot for comfort. Their two major titles were in direct conflict with National Magazines and IPC, and it was widely expected in the business that they would sell up. The favourite buyer was considered to be mighty IPC, but in the event they sold to Nat Mags. The German managing director, Holger Weiman, said that the company, although still profitable, was not large enough to compete in an increasingly tough and expensive marketplace. Media analysts showed no surprise at the sale: in their opinion it was a part of an inexorable wave of consolidation affecting not only magazine publishers but all the media, including retailing and wholesaling. Publishing companies were getting bigger, and it was considered an essential part of their business that they invest in new media, a financial burden which can take many years to show results on the balance sheet. Big was now beautiful, and Nat Mags gratefully absorbed G&J's five magazines into their portfolio of women's titles. The Germans had played a strategic role in developing the market in the 1980s and 1990s, particularly with the magical success of *Prima*, but the times were changing.

The ripples caused by the German sale were nothing compared to the earthquake which shook the foundations of magazine publishing the following year. IPC, the magazine conglomerate which had absorbed Hulton Press, George Newnes, Fleetway and Odhams and now published some hundred titles from their mini skyscraper on the South Bank, signed a £1.15 billion agreement with the American AOL Time Warner, creating the biggest transatlantic deal in magazine publishing. At a stroke a raft of famous titles, British household names, were surrendered to American control. This was great news for Michael Pepe, President and Chief Executive of Time Inc. International, who stated that IPC's reputation as a builder of brands and its position as market leader were the key factors in sealing the deal. 'We were looking to expand internationally as part of our corporate strategy, and one of the key markets is the UK,' said Mr Pepe. 'There was IPC, which is financially successful with a strong infrastructure, whose backers were known to be looking for an opportunity to exit. AOL Time Warner is a builder of brands. We love the magazine business, we love leaders. IPC is a leader and a builder of brands – we love IPC.'

If one can accept that this was a good deal for IPC – and in my opinion that is a very big 'if' – there can be no doubt that it was a hugely satisfying catch for Mr Pepe, who was like a man fishing for sardines who finds a whale in his net. Before the acquisition of IPC, Time Warner, which had been bought by the cable giant AOL, published only four magazines in Europe – *Time Europe*, *Fortune Europe*, *Wallpaper* and *In Style*, with a combined circulation of some 440,000. The British negotiator was Sly Bailey, IPC's lively Chief Executive, who was to leave the company after the sale and join Trinity Mirror.

The publishing industry was surprised and nervous about this deal, which many considered to be bad news in an already aggressively competitive market. Duncan Edwards of National Magazines, part of the American Hearst Corporation, said in a *Campaign* interview: 'I think it's business as usual. The things that are good about IPC, such as the weeklies, will continue to be good, while the things that are less good will continue to be less good.' But the Deputy Chief Executive of BBC Worldwide remarked to *Campaign*: 'AOL Time

Warner paid a full price for IPC, so it must be expecting great things. That should be enough of a warning for all of us.' The pygmies of the business must have been getting very anxious about their future.

Next in the gunsights was EMAP. A half-share in the successful British version of the magazine *Elle* had been purchased by EMAP in 1992. However, there was an interesting internecine struggle between EMAP and Hachette (now called Hachette Filipacchi), resulting in the latter taking over *Elle* in this country, as well as *Red, Top Santé* and *Psychologies*. Then EMAP was bought by the German company Bauer.

Currently, of the fifty top consumer magazines in the UK, thirty-seven are foreign-owned, and, of the top twenty-five women's lifestyle titles, twenty-two are in foreign ownership, as are seven out of ten men's lifestyle magazines and nine out of ten television listings magazines. As for celebrity magazines, six out of the ten leading titles are foreign, along with eight out of ten of the 'real-life' magazines. Even six out of eight film and music magazines have foreign owners. So it may surprise Mrs Brown of Tunbridge Wells to learn that her old favourites such as *Good Housekeeping, Woman's Own, Take a Break, Woman & Home, Woman's Weekly, Prima, Harper's Bazaar, Vogue* and *What's on TV* are all ultimately controlled from the USA or Germany, despite their British editorial and indigenous editors. But it may cheer her up to know that all the top children's magazines are British to the core.

Does it really matter if most of the UK's popular magazines are foreign owned? Probably not to their readers. The publishing companies are run reasonably independently, but all their budgets are determined abroad, which can affect the product. And the foreign-owned conglomerates cannot usually launch a new magazine in the UK without consultation and agreement from New York or Hamburg. When Bauer took over EMAP in 2007, forming themselves into Bauer Consumer Media, they took over a profitable stable of titles including

Closer, *Heat* and *Grazia*. But they immediately axed the struggling *New Woman* and *First*.

At least the UK's newspapers are domestically owned – or are they? The *Independent* is owned by the erstwhile Irish rugby player and Heinz tycoon Sir Anthony O'Reilly. The *Glasgow Herald* is owned by Gannett of the USA, and Johnson Press, owners of the *Scotsman* and the *Yorkshire Post*, have recently sold a 20 per cent stake in the company to a Malaysian billionaire; not forgetting that *The Times, Sunday Times* and the *Sun* are owned by an Australian. Even the dear old *Daily Telegraph* was controlled by the Canadian Conrad Black – before his incarceration; the owners are now the Barclay twins, who live in the Channel Islands.

6

THE NEW MILLENNIUM AND

THE CULT OF CELEBRITY

CELEBRITY TITLES DOMINATE THE BOOKSTALLS

–

NEWSPAPERS JOIN THE PARTY

–

THE NEW 'REALITY' GENRE

–

GLAMOUR SHOWS THAT SMALL IS BEAUTIFUL

–

THE TIMES GOES TABLOID

–

NEWSPAPERS FIGHT FOR CIRCULATION WITH
FREE GIFTS, PARTICULARLY DVDS

You need to button up your overcoat when you walk down Fleet Street these days. There is a distinct chill in the air – that gentle swishing noise you can hear is not falling leaves but falling circulations. And those chaps in baseball hats are not trying to sell you an evening paper: they are trying to give you a free copy to leave on the train when you have skimmed through their emaciated offering.

Nor is the temperature too hot in the palaces of the magazine tycoons. Their circulations are generally steady but at the expense of considerably discounted subscription selling. Some of the old favourites in the women's sector are getting creaky and losing favour, perhaps in some cases because their long-time fans are themselves falling off the shelves.

However, there is one sector upon which the sun continues to shine. It first saw the light of day in 1986, when the Spanish magazine *¡Hola!* was imported to the UK with the title *Hello!* There soon followed a rash of imitations, and the obsession with celebrity began to permeate the gossip columns of the red-top newspapers and even the news pages of the more august press. Gossip is as old as the hills, but this was more than just gossip: now 'stars' were instantly created out of nobodys, diary fodder out of nonentities. Overnight people – with or without talent or morals – were thrust into the media spotlight, exploited for all they were worth and then dropped again as quickly as they had been found.

¡Hola! had already enjoyed a successful career in Spain. The Spanish owners decided, rightly as it turns out, that the UK version would be equally successful since we are a nation of snobs, voyeurs, celebrity hunters and royalty enthusiasts. The magazine is printed in Spain with dramatically short print deadlines. The Editor in the UK, Maggie Goodman, the originator of *Company* magazine, announced in the first issue: 'We've all been educated over the last decades to appreciate the impact of colour, on television and in the cinema, so why shouldn't we expect the same standards when we turn to a magazine? Every picture tells a story and in *Hello!* we make sure we give enough space to cover the story in depth.' You can say that again! The magazine became famous, much to other publishers' amazement, for expending an enormous number of pages on a single story. The first issue, as we have seen, covered the wedding of Burt Reynolds. But would anyone in the business of newspapers and magazines back in 1988 have even begun to believe that in 2008 the sum of £500,000 would be paid to a minor royal for his wedding

pictures and that a magazine would stretch the story to a hundred pages? And who could have envisaged the Rooney story – a simple footballer's wedding – occupying three whole issues of the magazine and a payment to the newlyweds of £2.5 million? Or guessed that *Hello!* would pay £7 million for a picture of Brad Pitt's new-born baby?

Hello! and its close imitator *OK!* ran their circulations neck and neck for some time before the Spanish eased off, going for more advertising and a stable circulation around the 400,000 mark. *OK!*'s owner Richard Desmond went for many more rubber-necks and scandal-mongers, driving his circulation up to nearly 700,000. The magazine carries a satellite title called *Hot* which is piggy-backed in the other title. For £1.50 a copy you get about 260 pages of the stuff, definitely more bosh for your buck. There are no holds barred in this sort of publishing; competition is cut-throat in the constant search for scandalous pictures and infamous gossip. Cruelty often plays a big role in the mix. The titles all adore pictures of famous people of both sexes unsuccessfully waging private battles with their weight. As soon as stars appear on the world's beaches the secret cameras click, seeking out pot bellies, cellulite, sagging boobs, illicit trysts, unflattering or inappropriate clothes, outsize bums (they *love* outsize bums!), arcane tattoos, dire hairstyles, dramatic weight loss and, conversely, the ballooning of once attractive and admired figures. And the popular newspapers are right there, too. Were they so unkind in the days before the celeb magazines arrived?

A new sort of journalism had taken the country by storm. Women loved *Hello!* Here was the grapevine, the garden fence, the saucy rumour, the salacious story, all wrapped up in a large glossy magazine to be passed round the office. Celebrities, big or small, sometimes unknowns plucked from obscurity as a result of drunken liaisons in London nightclubs – all were grist to the celebrity mill.

The immediate competition came from Richard Desmond's Northern and Shell with *OK!* in 1993. It struggled in its early days against the might of *Hello!* but was to triumph as the battle went on. EMAP invented *Closer* to follow the success of *Heat*, which had started life poorly as an entertainment weekly but switched to enjoy the fruits of scandal. Not to be outdone, IPC brought out *Now*. (Did they forget the exclamation mark?) Northern and Shell launched *New!* and *Star*, while Nat Mags put their faith in *Reveal*. This new market was now accounting for some 7 million copies every week. You have to admire the publishers' inventiveness in digging out all those celebs, mini-celebs and non-celebs every week. In this task they had reciprocal assistance from the red-top newspapers.

Weekly magazines have the problem of topicality. Today's Big Bum can be yesterday's news by the time the magazine goes to press, if it has been seen in all its obesity and obscenity in the red-tops a couple of days before. The search is always on for exclusive deals with the paparazzi, and of course the newspapers have Fleet Street budgets, the ability to pay more and publish fast. Still, not every celebrity story has to be a major newsflash: there are acres of pictures and features about dull 'personalities' who have often invented themselves through their public relations manipulators. Most of them are not front-page news in the old journalistic sense – if you are not glued to the telly hour by hour you can be completely baffled who many of them are.

The magazines are always on the look-out for weddings, tying up exclusives for mouth-watering sums of money. The £2.5 million paid by *OK!* for the Rooney wedding seems a quite baffling sum for a magazine to splash out on a single feature, but Richard Desmond also owns the *Daily Express*, the *Sunday Express*, the *Daily Star* and the other celebrity titles *Star* and *New!*, so he could manufacture spin-offs all round. The word in the trade was that Desmond made a killing out of extra sales across all his titles, and he actually spun the wedding out over three issues of *OK!*.

A perpetual preoccupation with diet runs through most of the titles. Thin is in, cuddly is out. The word 'diet' on the front cover is a winner, together with that devilish word 'cellulite'. The magazines are here to show us who fails to sustain the ideal shape. *Now* (the IPC offering, if you are in danger of getting confused) ran a feature 'What I Ate Today' in which a famous icon, or even a TV presenter, would detail her daily food intake from breakfast to dinner, complete with calorie count and expert's advice. *Reveal*, from Nat Mags, likes to employ the euphemism 'dimpled thighs' when discussing the dreaded cellulite. The magazines seem particularly keen on beach shots that show their captured celebrities to best disadvantage.

Whatever the merits of the genre, the celebrity cult has created an entire industry for editorial staff (I hold back from the term 'journalists') and photographers and helps the supermarkets shovel out the products the magazines advertise. Of course the red-top newspapers encourage the celebrity titles and vice versa, driving each other's standards downwards in the process. The TV series *Big Brother* is a constant source of distasteful copy, together with other programmes such as *I'm a Celebrity, Get Me Out of Here*. It is interesting to read Hugh Cudlipp in 1988 (quoted by Ruth Dudley Edwards in her book *Newspapermen*) on the subject of the downmarket plunge of the *Daily Mirror* in the teeth of increasingly populist editorial in the *Sun*:

> It was the dawn of the Dark Ages of tabloid journalism, the decades, still with us, when the proprietors and the editors – not all, but most – decided that playing a continual role in public enlightenment was no longer any business of the popular Press.

Information about foreign affairs was relegated to a three-inch yapping editorial insulting foreigners.

It was the age when investigative journalism in the public interest shed its integrity and became intrusive journalism for the prurient, when nothing, however personal, was any longer secret or sacred and the basic human right to privacy was banished in the interest of publishing profit – when bingo became a new journalistic art form when the daily nipple count and the sleazy stories about bonking bimbos achieved a dominant influence in the circulation charts.

I find it deplorable when the red-top newspapers splash a story about some unfortunate celebrity on the front page. The assumption that the reader recognizes the personality, often referred to by some matey sobriquet, is rather presumptuous and puzzling to many of us less aware citizens. For instance, many people, particularly fruiterers, may have been puzzled by this front-page headline from the *Sun* in July 2008:

PEACHES IN DRUG OVERDOSE

It reminded me of one of my favourite headlines from *The Times*, on 30 May 2000, when Canaan Banana, Zimbabwe's former President, lost his appeal against conviction for a series of sexual offences:

BANANA LOSES SODOMY APPEAL

The red-top newspapers are not the only offenders in their exploitation of the celebrity cult. The diary pages of the quality and mid-market dailies are not above seizing on a PR-inspired photograph of some well-known person at a routine social event. There are occasions when the personality becomes the main topic. For instance, in June 2008 the London *Evening Standard* devoted more space on its front page to a picture of Kate Moss at some event with her boyfriend than it gave to the headline story about the first woman solider to be killed in Afghanistan.

The popular press has been moving inexorably for many years into the realm once monopolized by the women's magazines. Health, beauty, fashion, gossip, agony aunts, hairdressing, plastic surgery – all are fully covered day by day. Even the august *Times* has mutated the 'Times 2' section into pages with a strong female interest. Naturally, the Fleet Street editor will want to appeal to the interests of both sexes, but the newspapers' expansion into the female domain has surely been a factor in the declining circulations of many of the traditional women's weekly magazines.

Celebrity magazines are not to be confused with the self-styled 'reality' titles. As the name suggests, these are magazines which tell true stories. In simpler days they had titles like *True Romances* and *True Story*, although their veracity was often in doubt. The new breed are much more earthy, with stories such as 'My mother had a baby by my fiancé!' and 'My nose ate itself . . . shocking pictures inside' and various sexual complications. The magazines pay money to the readers who submit a published true story and, to judge by examples seen, the more bizarre the better. The going rate appears to be £500, and the story can be phoned, faxed, emailed or even posted. The market leader is *Take a Break*, which EMAP Bauer publish. Others are *That's Life,* also from Bauer, and IPC's *Pick Me Up* and *Chat*. The titles are full of puzzles, prize-winning competitions, health stories (they love the rude bits) and all the usual content of traditional women's magazines. The divide between 'reality' and 'traditional' is extremely thin, which may also help to explain the falling circulations of the older titles. Murdoch's News International had a small piece of the reality market with *Love It!* but withdrew in 2008 as the sales were failing. At the same time they announced in *The Times* that they were going to 'offload the Sky customer magazine either to BSB or a third party whilst retaining the *Sunday Times Travel Magazine*'. The editorial piece ended: 'Further launches will not take place.' This was the second time that Murdoch had withdrawn from the magazine business. The reality magazine sector is in any case probably not capable of much expansion.

As the cliché tells us, size isn't everything. Over the years, magazines have come in all shapes and sizes, with pocket titles occasionally proving popular. The only magazine consistently to pursue the pocket path has been *Reader's Digest*, which these days is a shadow of its former glorious self. So it was interesting that Condé Nast launched *Glamour* in 2001 in a pocket or handbag format. They had found the small format very popular when they launched the title in Italy. The new magazine scored an immediate hit, with its circulation soaring past *Cosmopolitan* and settling down to an impressive 550,000. Women apparently loved the smaller size, even if they never actually put it in their handbags. Because publishers love originality and individuality, several of Condé Nast's rivals instantly copied them, producing small-sized alternatives to their own titles, including *Cosmopolitan* itself. Little editions now sat on the bookstalls alongside their bigger sisters.

The newspaper world also began to downsize, partly to save paper but partly in reaction to reader demand. Old colonels in Pall Mall clubs were amazed, but generally pleased, to find their copy of *The Times* had shrunk in the wash: tabloid was the new format for most of the papers. There were stubborn reactionaries: the *Daily* and *Sunday Telegraphs* and the mighty *Sunday Times* are still broadsheet and seem to have no plans to reduce. Another exception was the *Guardian*, which took its time to change but favoured what they called the Berliner form.

This is not quite a tabloid and not quite a broadsheet – a bit like Churchill's remark when someone told him a man was named Bossom: 'It's neither one thing nor another!' Readers do like the tabloid size, which is easier to handle when you're trying to open the paper in a crowded railway carriage or at the breakfast table.

The first decade of the new millennium was not a dynamic period for the national newspapers, despite some fiddling with new layouts, ceaseless free gifts of DVDs of old films and the arcane technique of bulk sales and subscriptions. Circulations remained obstinately static or declining. The expansion of the battle of free newspapers in the streets added to the confusion, as did the forward march of the internet with a proliferation of websites from the newspapers themselves. The internecine competition as intense as ever.

The magazine business faced its own problems, with falling readerships and increasing costs. They put a lot of faith in subscription selling, as we will see. But this section of the media is for ever reinventing itself, launching, relaunching and closing. Before the sell-out to the German Bauer, EMAP aimed at a difficult market sector when it launched the Italian fashion magazine *Grazia* in the UK. This is a spiky area, dominated by *Vogue* and the UK version of *Elle*. But the newcomer was a quick success, attaining a sale of 230,000. *Grazia* is a glossy weekly with popular fashion and, it has to be added, a strong element of 'celebrity'. IPC spent a big budget (after having 'researched the market for some years') on the launch of their new weekly *Look* (an unoriginal name), which did well by selling 300,000 copies and was soon claiming on the cover to be 'Britain's Best Selling Weekly'. At £1.40 with a varnished cover, it touted itself as the first high street fashion and celebrity weekly. However, much to the chagrin of the rest of the glossy fashion press, *Grazia* was named 'media icon of our times' by the Periodical Publishers' Association in their annual awards.

Burda, another giant German printing and publishing company, apparently felt that if Bauer could get a foothold in the UK, so could they. They thought their teenage magazine *Young Lisa* could do well here, although they wisely changed the name to *Amber*. They dubbed it confusingly 'the youngest glossy lifestyle magazine for women' and claimed that 16- to 22-year-old women was a sector that 'has considerable under-exploited potential'. Given such a misjudgement, it is not surprising that the magazine soon folded. So did that popular 1969 football magazine for boys and grown-up boys, *Shoot*, which was for a while the most popular footie magazine in the country with sales of over 120,000. The referee's whistle blew in 2008, leaving the field to *Match*.

Imitate and attack are the watchwords in magazine publishing, so Condé Nast launched *Easy Living* in 2005 aiming directly at the old-established auntie of magazines *Good Housekeeping*, even poaching the publisher of that magazine. Condé Nast was once the sleeping giant of the glossies, gently but profitably snoring away for many years while IPC and Nat Mags were launching new titles. However, the success of *Vanity Fair* and the resurrection of *Tatler* had spurred them into action with the highly successful launch of *Glamour*. *Easy Living* is colour-coded for easy reference, but progress has been slow and the sales are some quarter of a million behind the mature but still lively *Good Housekeeping*.

The fashion bible, otherwise known as *Vogue*, is still the top glossy in the UK, well ahead of its old transatlantic rival *Harper's Bazaar*, which has suffered a name change from *Harper's & Queen*. I may be biased, but the dropping of the emotive '*Queen*' from the title surely removed some distinction and reader familiarity, and after thirty-eight years of brand building the change to the more mundane name is in danger of condemning the magazine to be simply a runner-up to *Vogue*.

The newspapers were getting into the world of give-aways and offers to maintain precarious circulations. The *Mail*, in particular, relied on the free DVD as an added incentive to buy the paper, for both the daily and the Sunday. The Saturday editions of most of the papers felt that some sort of freebee was a necessary inducement, particularly as cover prices were creeping up. Magazines had followed a similar path back in the early 1990s when cover-mounts were all the rage, indeed almost obligatory. *BBC Gardening World* attached a free trug to their cover, while IPC's *Your Garden* included a pair of gardening gloves worth £1.50, a generous inducement when the magazine cost £1.45. *Practical Fishkeeping* attached a bag of pond food, *Slimming* a chocolate-chip bar, *Parents* a tube of moisturizing cream and *Your Horse* a pack of Pedigree Chum Schmackos. *Mother and Baby* went for a feeding spoon, *Amateur Photographer* a film box, *Today's Golfer* a golf towel and *Trailfinder* a useful survival bag. The classic was *Home and Freezer Digest*, which attached a bag of instant mashed potato, obliterating the cover itself. It was not long before the cover-mount game was up except for special (desperate) occasions. Of course, the newspapers have found that a DVD is a slim gift, easily tucked into a plastic bag inside a paper's supplement, so they may be here to stay, even when they have exhausted the repertoire of old films.

Newspaper reader incentives go back to the 1930s. When Odhams Press took over full control of the *Daily Herald* in 1929 it embarked on a desperate campaign to move the circulation up to an ambitious 2 million. It sent out a sales force of door-to-door canvassers offering bribes of free cameras and other goodies if the householder signed up to the *Herald*. It offered readers the whole set Dickens's novels, an offer quickly copied by some of the other dailies. Fleet Street papers even tried selling insurance policies. There is nothing new, as you might say, under the *Sun*.

8

THE AGE OF THE FREEBIES

THE RISE OF THE FREE NEWSPAPER

–

FREE EVENINGS DO BATTLE ON THE STREETS OF
LONDON

–

NEWSPAPER SELLERS ARE LESS THAN IMPRESSED

–

IS THIS THE FUTURE?

If you live in a big city you grow accustomed to the commercialization of street life. People try to sell you things, such as a copy of the *Big Issue* or a charity flag. A recent nuisance has been gangs of 'chuggers', or charity muggers, endeavouring to sign you up to endless direct debits for charity. The skilful city dweller learns to avoid the pitfalls. If you are old enough you may remember, after the Second World War, the plague of street photographers who would snap you as you walked along the street, take your money and post a blurred picture on to you. Perhaps more of a surprise to a young person teleported back in time to the 1950s would be the overt prostitution that plagued London's West End. A walk through Curzon Street and its environs would find almost every corner or doorway occupied by a lady with a hard sell.

We all buy the *Big Issue*, at least when our eyes are caught. We must do so, because its circulation has reached an impressive 176,000

copies, which is pretty good going. And when you get your magazine home you may be surprised to discover that the editorial can be
incisive and challenging.

These days publishers also want to give you some of their products for free. This is not new thinking – the first free title I can trace
was called *Modern Living with Gas* which was posted to all customers
of North Thames Gas back in 1938. This was targeted publishing,
which was also the notion behind the free magazines for office girls
handed out at London tube stations for some years from the early
1970s. The selection of potential readers was easy: the magazine was
given to young and youngish girls hurtling past on their way to the
office. The advertising was mainly for situations vacant, hordes of
clerical and secretarial jobs, supported by cheap flights and holidays.
Haymarket was quick off the mark with *West One*, to be swiftly
followed by *Girl about Town* and *Ms London*. Their success or failure
depended on the conscientious identification of the potential reader
(not always the case) and, of course, a satisfactory response for the
advertisers. This was a great idea when the job market was booming
and the internet as yet unknown.

Local free newspapers, usually delivered door to door, became
popular – at least with the publishers. Local jobs, shops, entertainment facilities and services provided the advertising in competition
with the traditional paid-for local newspapers. The difference to the
reader was the quality and extent of the editorial, although advertisers were happy if they got the right response. Generally in the early
days free newspapers were of poor journalistic quality.

Free magazines, usually of professional standard, became increasingly acceptable in the 1970s. Estate agents were quick to seize on the
possibility of their own titles distributed door to door, and these
magazines became more sophisticated over the years. Supermarkets
came to realize the potential of own brand titles, as did some of the

major London department stores. So 'free' and 'give-away' were no longer pejorative words. Many mail-order catalogues also became magazine-like.

It was into this environment that Associated Newspapers, publishers of the *Daily Mail* and the London *Evening Standard*, decided to launch *Metro*, their free morning paper which sits in stands at tube and mainline stations. The commuter can take a copy off the stand, and if all the copies have vanished, which they do at some stations very quickly, you can usually pick one up on the train when the previous reader has left it on his or her seat. This is the age of the throw-away – you seldom take the paper on to the office. *Metro*, launched in 1999, has become part of the London commuter experience, alongside cattle-truck congestion. According to the International Media Consulting Group in their 2008 *Innovations in Newspapers World Report*, the UK *Metro* is the second largest free newspaper in the world with a daily distribution of 1.35 million copies across the country. According to the report,

> The free-sheets have attracted a huge new audience to newspapers, one that is heavily female, and younger than the average newspaper readers, with a demographic similar to that of television. Advertisers recognize this new market. Readers like the clean design and lay-outs and the lack of editorial opinion meant that the papers could not clash with a reader's point of view.

The report concluded that the distribution model of the free-sheets had been a real success.

> One key advantage of the free press has been its ability to bypass the rigid and often atrophied distribution channels of the paid press . . . handing out papers at stations and on the street leaves

people with little choice but to pick up the paper and start reading.
Free distribution seeks the reader rather than the traditional pattern
of readers seeking the newspaper.

The report's enthusiasm came with a caveat, however: 'Free papers
cannot survive when four or more large-circulation titles chase the
same advertisers and readers in the same place.'

I expected a big reaction from the newsagents, particularly the
stalwarts who own the station bookstall kiosks. I asked the man who
runs the news-stand at our local Underground station for his opinion.
Had the sales of his morning papers taken a dip? He told me that they
hadn't and that he still sold the same quantities of the *Telegraph*, *The
Times* and the others as he had done before the *Metro* invasion. I said
it must be a bit galling to see the free-sheets given away in front of his
nose. Had he ever complained, as many other non-newsagent
retailers would do if goods were being given away outside their
shops? He shrugged his shoulders. 'What can we do? They wouldn't
take any notice of us.'

Over the years the advertising in *Metro* has developed in both
quantity and variety. Broadband and mobile phone advertisements
dominate, followed by cheap airlines and financial inducements. The
classified columns are filled with situations vacant and educational
courses. Of course, if the advertising did *not* grow the whole operation
would collapse – unless Lord Rothermere is an altruist. Whether the
quality of the display advertising is also growing is not as evident.
Sheer mass and weight of numbers never create an attractive environment for the more sophisticated advertisers, and the free distribution
method is very much a blunderbuss approach, scattering its shot all
over the place, horizontally and not vertically. None the less the free
newspaper movement is now a *fait accompli*: there are over two
hundred titles in fifty-five countries worldwide. Alongside the

The business editorial is international and comprehensive. The paper lets its hair down on Saturdays when it publishes an excellent weekend section. Circulation is an impressive 450,000. The launch of the free-sheet *City AM* does not seem to have dented sales.

- *Guardian* It decided to be neither fish nor fowl when it opted for the Berliner format, avoiding the move to bog-standard tabloid. The new shape is rather curious but serviceable when you get used to it. Having said that, every day there is also *G2*, which is a tabloid section with profiles, the arts, telly listings and puzzles, protecting the purity of the main paper from the invasion of trivia. *G2* also carries a readable section called 'Review of Reviews', which sums up the opinions of critics from the other papers. The main paper carries all the leading features you would expect the *Guardian* to carry, with liberal overtones. Every Monday there is a media section which is the most comprehensive in the daily press, stuffed with situations vacant from the media. Saturday contains a weekend magazine plus the usual leisure sections. The circulation of the paper is 350,000, with a median age of 45. The male/female readership ratio is 57/43.

- *Independent* This has the lowest circulation in the 'quality press' at 240,000. It aims at the young ABC1 market and has attained a median readership age of 43. It carries a media section on Mondays, a property section on Wednesdays and the inevitable weekend magazine on Saturdays. It is also big on education and careers, with a weekly section on Thursdays. The sex ratio is 62/38.

- *Daily Sport* This is as near as you can get to a daily men's magazine masquerading as a newspaper. It sells 85,000 copies every day at a cover price of 50p, is stuffed with bottoms and boobs and pages of advertisements for sex aids and sexual contacts. Otherwise it carries no display advertising. The editorial makes the *Sun* and the *Daily Star* look like the traditional vicar's tea party. Don't buy it for Auntie under the impression that it's the *Racing Post*.

- **London Evening Standard** This is not a national daily, and it only appears five days a week, but to most thinking Londoners it is an unmissable read. At its best the *Standard* is the complete evening read, national and local at the same time. It officially sells 300,000, but 'bulks' are involved. At 50p it has a hard road to climb in the teeth of all the competing free-sheets, including its own mini-*doppelgänger* called *Lite*. It publishes a 'Homes and Property' section on Wednesday and a socially conscious toffs' colour magazine on Friday, which always seems at odds with the paper, including *Tatler*-style party photographs. Until a few years ago it published a Thursday entertainment magazine with all the London listings, which seems a more relevant use of the newsprint.

Our national dailies are pretty uniform. The four 'qualities', *The Times*, *Telegraph*, *Independent* and *Guardian*, run similar stories every day. Many of the features are, of course, duplicated: reviews, obituaries, letters, financial sections, crosswords, sudoku, the back pages of sport, business sections and so on. Even the columnists run to a pattern: the grouchy, the light-hearted, the astringent, the nostalgic. You pays your money; you takes your choice. We tend to grow comfortable with our daily paper, we know our way around and we enjoy particular columnists and most likely agree with the political slant. The same can be said of the two 'mid-markets', the

Mail and the *Express*. The two more respectable red-tops, the *Sun* and the *Mirror*, are rather more interchangeable (except for the tits), and the *Daily Star* and the *Sport* are in their own league.

Do we need so many national dailies, if they are so similar? Can they all survive in the years of gloom and doom being forecast by the financial pundits?

With these questions buzzing in our minds, let us have a look at the state of our eleven national Sundays.

- *Sunday Times* This sometimes all seems to be written by A.A. Gill, with his astringent wit. It used to claim, until recently, that 'the *Sunday Times* is the Sunday papers'. Launched in 1822, it comes in multiple sections – generating good business for osteopaths who specialize in treating Sunday newsboys. The paper's profile is good: circulation 1.2 million, readership 3 million, median age 45, male/female ratio 55/45 and North/South split 40/60. But the paper weighs a heavy armful, and the cover price was recently raised to a record £2. This resulted in a circulation slip of some 3 per cent. Then came a great make-over, coinciding with a relocation of the printing operation to Hertfordshire. As the Editor declaimed: 'For the first time in its history, every page of every section of this news-paper can be printed in full colour.' The new slogan to represent the paper became 'For all you are'. This has baffled people, since it is indeed the sort of meaningless waffle that advertising agents could apply to almost any product. The biggest innovation is that the paper is now colour-coded so the dull-witted can find their way around. The main criticism still applies: there are too many sections, too much paper, it is very unwieldy, too heavy, with too many advertising insets. Do we need three magazines plus nine sections?

- *Sunday Telegraph* Launched in 1961, this paper sells 619,000 copies with a readership of 1.7 million. It follows the section formula of the *Sunday Times*, with a main paper, sport, business, travel, home/living, money/jobs, the colour magazine and a style magazine called *Stella*. It is, like the daily, a broadsheet with a median readership age of 56 and a sex ratio of 55/45. Readership is geographically heavily biased, with a North/South ratio of 30/70. The paper has a workmanlike appearance and performance without the bulkiness of its rival. The colour magazine is rather limp and a lot of the pages are the week's TV listings. Comparisons are always odious, but it is fair to say that *The Times* generally has more bite. I get the impression that the *Telegraphs* are taken by people who might prefer the 'other one' but who disapprove of Mr Murdoch.

- *Observer* Berliner-sized like its sister daily, the *Guardian*, this is our oldest Sunday newspaper, launched in 1791. It reaches a relatively young market, with a median age of 43 and a core readership of AB adults aged 25–44. It is balanced in its sex ratio, with 52 per cent male readers and 48 per cent female. There is a colour magazine and a separate TV listings section. The holiday section is called 'Escape'. It carries a series of monthly magazine sections such as 'Food', 'Music', 'Sport' and 'Observer Woman'. It has one of the best critics sections of all the Sundays. Overall it makes a neat, readable package. If you are a *Guardian* reader you will like this Sunday. Circulation is 428,000.

- *Independent on Sunday* Launched in 1990, this one comes in a 'compact' size (slightly larger than the tabloids) and come. This is a sub-industry of immense energy. All Desmond needs is plenty of high-profile weddings.

None the less I deplore the lack of originality shown by today's magazines publishing business. Where are the big ideas, the innovative new launches?

11

WHITHER THE PRINT MEDIA?

THE PRINT MEDIA MUST COME TO TERMS
WITH THE ELECTRONIC AGE, AS THE
DIGITAL MARKET GROWS APACE

–

THE YOUNG ARE THE NEWSPAPERS' FUTURE,
BUT THE PAPERS THEMSELVES ARE MIDDLE-AGED

–

WILL ALL NEWSPAPERS BECOME GIVE-AWAYS?

–

WILL THE SUPERMARKETS DOMINATE DISTRIBUTION?

–

WILL THE NEWSAGENTS SURVIVE?

Not bogeymen but search engines stalk the restless dreams of press barons. Google is the new six-letter word, liable to bring sales executives out in a cold sweat. A whole new lexicon has appeared: platforms, on line, websites, blogs, social networking, Yahoo (wasn't that a repulsive creature from *Gulliver's Travels*?) . . .

Having more or less solved technological problems associated with producing printed publications, the press now finds itself confronted by an entirely new wave of technological challenges. The internet has changed the face of communication and has been taken up with fervour by the young. We used to send off cheques in response to advertisers; consumers now coolly book on line, and both buyer and seller enjoy a quick deal. Press advertising is suddenly passé.

Or is it? The press world must have taken cheer when in the middle of 2008 the Advertising Association announced that for the year 2007 press advertising (newspapers and magazines) was the biggest medium, netting a heart-warming £7.1 billion. Before anyone reaches for the Moët, however, the figure for the internet showed an increase year on year of 40 per cent. The Futures Director of GroupM media communications agency, Adam Smith, has forecast that internet advertising spending will overtake television in 2009. Looking further ahead, media agency Zenith Optimedia has prophesied that in 2010 internet spend will hit £4.36 billion. To put the boot in a bit more, Zenith confidently states that online display advertising will attract more revenue than consumer magazines, radio or outdoor advertising by that year.

Then again, the world has always been a tough place for the print media. Competition has come from the cinema, television, outdoor advertising, radio and a never-ending flow of new magazines. The major publishers of newspapers and magazines have taken the bull by the horns and leaped on the website bandwagon. You can tell how important the newspapers view their websites because they have started scrapping about the figures. The electronic arm of the Audit Bureau of Circulations verifies claims of hits on websites. The Telegraph.co.uk has claimed 18,646,112 unique users in the UK and worldwide, with the Guardian.co.uk and Mail Online following with over 18 million users each; Timesonline reached 15 million, and the Sun recorded a mere 14 million. At the time of writing there is some scepticism about the figures.

Peter Preston, once the Editor of the *Guardian* and now a media commentator, made an interesting point in the *Observer* on 13 July 2008: 'We know the internet is part of the future, because we are most passionately told so . . . but we don't know how it will fare in recession.'

7

SUBSCRIPTIONS ARE THE NEW GAME

MAGAZINE SUBSCRIPTIONS BALLOON
–
NEWSAGENTS COME OFF SECOND BEST
–
NEWSPAPERS FOLLOW SUIT WITH CUT-PRICE
OFFERS AND FREE DELIVERY

Time was when buying a magazine subscription was an awkward and clumsy operation for both the magazine and the potential subscriber – in fact so clumsy that it was not considered a practicable publishing tool. You could always buy a subscription to any magazine, of course, particularly if you wanted copies sent to Auntie Doris up in the Orkneys who was rather devoid of a local John Menzies or to dear old Uncle Bill who was still running his tobacco farm in Matabele country. You would be charged the entire cost of the postage, and the title would eventually arrive at its destination. But when it did arrive it would be rolled up in a wrapper which the recipient had to open by tearing a strip along one side, usually taking a few edges of the magazine with it. Then the magazine would have to be unrolled to become readable, but the roll was often obdurate, creating a permanently curled magazine.

Then the polythene wrapper was invented. This meant that the magazine would be inserted flat, would mail flat and arrive flat.

Even if the postman folded the package up to insert it in the letter-box it would unfold itself as it landed on the doormat. Bliss! Cunning publishers understood the potential: other things could be popped in the plastic envelope. These could include letters from the publisher offering deals or advertisers' leaflets known as inserts. A new commercial era had arrived, the chance to exploit the 'brand extension' for the publishers and their advertisers. Printers were obliged to introduce new machinery for magazine wrapping and inserting, and publishers realized that if subscription services were to become a necessary function of building circulations the bought subscription should be given the advantage of earlier receipt than the same issue purchased at the newsagent.

The news trade was very sensitive about publishers selling magazines directly in this way. It was very galling for Mr Patel, your friendly local newsagent, to open his copies, delivered by the wholesaler, and find an advertisement or a loose insert suggesting that readers could order the magazines by subscription and not just save money but receive their copies before they reached the newsagent. Supermarkets will not accept loose inserts in their copies, blaming our old friends Health and Safety: somebody might slip up on a dropped glossy inset and sue the supermarket. But most subscription advertisements are on the page these days, so that problem is largely eradicated.

The news trade moaned and complained and threatened and sulked, but there was little they could do. Some newsagents would go through the magazines and shake out the subscription leaflets, but this was time-consuming, and they could not censor advertisements printed in the pages of the magazines. There were also direct-mail campaigns and cross-promotions through the other magazines in the group, so a *Vogue* reader, for instance, would be offered a lure to buy *Tatler*. The new subscription offers would always contain a financial bait. Not only would your copy of *Good Housekeeping* arrive a couple of days before Mrs Jenkins next door could buy hers at the local shop but you would be paying less for the product as well.

Of course these financial offers were not an altruistic gesture by the publishing trade. The advertising market was getting tough, competition was extensive, not only from other magazines or newspapers but also from the new world of the internet. Magazine cover prices were increasing, sometimes to extravagant levels, to keep up with rises in the cost of paper and print, and potential buyers were hardly short of choice in buying other publications if they thought your cover price was exorbitant. Under these circumstances a subscription offer could be attractive to the buyer and affordable to the publisher, who needed subscriptions to bolster circulation. Moreover, higher cover prices went some way to mollifying the newsagents, who were taking a 25 per cent share of a higher figure. Trebles all round, as *Private Eye* would say! Other factors driving this trend were the spread of internet commerce and the now-ubiquitous direct debit, a useful and profitable tool for all purveyors of goods and services. Publishers rely on the routine and – let it be whispered – the forgetfulness of the subscriber. Once a direct debit is made out subscribers will forget, or not bother, to cancel their subscriptions.

Although one prominent magazine publisher has told me that it takes three years for magazine subscriptions to become profitable, they have become the lifeblood of the business. The same publisher confessed quietly that it is not unknown for a magazine to reduce the paper quality in the subscription copies, thus saving paper costs and postage weight, but this is generally imperceptible to the reader.

A successful subscription drive is a 'win–win' strategy for the publisher. He (or she) builds up the circulation base by proselytizing in his own magazine, avoiding expensive media costs, and takes the whole revenue from the subscription. He saves the 25 per cent the retailer takes and 45 per cent distribution costs. He has to cut the subscription rate featured in the offer but can probably increase it later as the subscription settles down. Armed with a substantial subscription figure he can make his print order each month in the comfortable knowledge that he has firm sales, whereas the sales estimate of copies sold through the trade might be subject to discount and returns.

The flood gates have certainly opened on the subscription bonanza. At one time magazines bothered only with a token sale of gift subscriptions, suggesting that a quality monthly made a novel Christmas gift for Auntie ('Beryl says Merry Christmas and remembers you every month of the year'). *Good Housekeeping* built a steady subscription base of 14,000 copies using this approach. Today subscriptions to *Good Housekeeping* exceed 220,000, nearly equalling all the sales in the news trade and supermarkets. Other recent examples of subscription offers include the following:

- *Harper's Bazaar* entices you by cutting its subscription by £29 in addition to offering free hand and nail cream, plus hand polish worth £45.
- *House Beautiful* offers twelve issues for £18.60, a discount of 50 per cent.
- *Esquire* gives you one year's issues for £15, a saving of £32.88.
- *Viz* offers three issues for £1 plus *Viz* golf balls and 21 per cent discount on every ten issues.
- *Saga* magazine has a privileged subscription of only £5.95 for twelve issues or £9.95 for twenty-four, a saving of £50.05, as well as a free draw for a holiday.
- *Time* is very generous by direct mail. Instead of £151.20, you pay £20.00 for fifty-four issues, plus a 1 GB USB stick, plus special issues.

- *Private Eye* offers 50 per cent off the annual subscription by direct debit.
- *Vogue* (yes, even *Vogue!*) will give you twelve issues for £39 plus a free gift of skin care and two extra free gifts if you pay by direct debit.
- *Easy Living* makes life easier by giving you twelve issues for £18, a saving of £14.
- *She* has 'massive saving' of 69 per cent, with £3.30 copies for £1 each.
- *Tatler* offers a free gift worth £38.
- *Country Living* will give you two free books from the Richard and Judy Book Club.

The ideal for a magazine publisher would be to achieve a total subscription circulation: no messing about with a distributor, wholesaler or retailer. Every single copy would be pre-bought and posted – the bookstall means nothing to you. This way of selling also suggests the image of an exclusive club of readers, an interesting concept for advertisers if the club is composed of the sort of people they are after. One publication that lives this dream is *Saga* magazine, which has a very definite reader profile of over-45s. This is the 'grey market', the older reader who may be retired and has leisure time and, in theory, the financial wherewithal to purchase holidays, insurance, stair lifts, funeral plans and other goodies that may appeal to the not-so-young. *Saga* can proudly boast that it has 651,000 actively purchased subscriptions with an affluent audience of over-45s, with 100 per cent home delivery and an official readership of nearly 2 million. This circulation performance leaves EMAP Bauer's *Yours* magazine way down the street with half that figure and must worry *Reader's Digest*, too.

Saga carries out continuous and aggressive selling of its subscriptions, waving very generous and tempting offers at potential buyers.

Obviously the title depends heavily on its circulation, and once they've got you they want to hang on to you. They also have the advantage of a holiday company which can constantly pump new names into the subscription pot. This is a professional organization, and the magazine has seen an impressive and much-needed improvement in editorial and design quality. It is in the enviable position of cornering the market for the older customer, and it is particularly powerful now that it has merged with the Automobile Association. In 2007, before the merger, *Saga* enjoyed sales revenue from all its products of £688 million. The magazine is a very effective marketing tool, devoting much space to holidays, health care and so on, so it gets the wrinkly audience one way or another.

There is another method of convincing buyers that they should subscribe to your magazine – door-to-door selling. This can be a minefield, as I discovered back in 1970 when we had relaunched *Harper's Bazaar*. My managing director had met a rather dodgy, monocled ex-major at a party in the House of Commons who convinced him that he had the organization to bump up fully paid-for subscriptions with doorstep selling. This was tempting as *Harper's* was suffering from low sales after a few years of neglect. The major demanded an eye-wateringly hefty commission, but the situation was rather dire and we gave him the go-ahead. Within weeks the complaints started to come in, with many telephone enquiries to ask if we really were selling the magazine in such a fashion and would buyers really receive the copies they paid for. We then discovered that the sales team was made up of young, indigent Australian world travellers anxious to get some quick money. They all adopted the same sales approach, which was virtually a sob-story, telling the prospective subscriber that their mother was dying of cancer back in Australia and they desperately needed the commission to be able to fly home and see the grey-haired old lady before she expired. As the publisher,

I got the flak, and I was justifiably excoriated by Esther Rantzen, then the fraud investigator for the *Bernard Braden Show*. We immediately called a halt to the scam, and the major disappeared.

Publishers can also buy lists for their mail sales campaigns to bolster subscriptions. This can engender furious phone calls from people demanding to know how their names were obtained. None the less direct mail is a useful tool in building circulation, and expert communicators such as *Time*, *Newsweek* and the *Economist* have employed it successfully for years.

Of course, the king of the subscription game is *Reader's Digest*, the little pocket magazine. They have always worked hard at building their subscription base to sell the magazine and their varied books. The popular myth is that once you are on the list you never get off, even unto death. They are still running their sweepstake: today as I write I have just received my offer. 'Today in your area we're inviting fewer than 2 per cent of households to take part. So very few, if any, of your neighbours are as lucky as you . . . Enter the next draw and you're in – if you want to be the winner of £250,000.' Nothing to buy, nothing to sign up to. But over the months the lucky chosen recipient will receive a number of offers to buy books with 'yes' and 'no' envelopes. I am told that a large manila *Reader's Digest* envelope bearing a unique tracking reference is due to arrive at my house. I have seventy-two hours to make up my mind. It is jolly nice of them to think of me, and many thousands of people will almost certainly take up the opportunity. However, the magazine, so small you want to cuddle it, has been going through hard times. The circulation is down to about 600,000 and has been declining for years, although their readership, according to industry figures, is still over a million. Their mailing operation and persistent selling techniques are probably unrivalled in this country. They can certainly shift books if not the magazine these days.

Another publishing strategy for building sales is the give-away – offering free copies by post if you reply to an advertisement in the press. If you do so, you will receive a free copy in the mail complete with the suggestion that you will most likely wish to purchase a subscription. Or you can do what Condé Nast did with *Glamour* in December 2007, according to *Marketing Week* magazine. They 'piggy-backed' copies of the magazine with their other magazine, *Easy Living*. The two titles are not especially synergistic in their readerships or their editorial, but every little helps, as the supermarket says. *Glamour* is also keen on cover-mounts (four a year, according to the publisher) to boost sales figures. But the magazine has made a successful entrée into *Cosmopolitan* country, outselling the 1972 title by 90,000 copies although lagging behind in readership figures.

The subscription market is here to stay. Many famous monthly magazines are working towards a subscription base of 50 per cent of their circulation. Weekly magazines are not such an attractive subscription proposition because of the time factor, but the *Economist*, the *Spectator* and recently the *Radio Times* have all been taking an interest in developing postal sales. Overall, 13.5 per cent of all consumer magazines are now sold on subscription, with thousands of professional and specialized magazines relying on the Royal Mail. And there could be the snag. We have seen the irrational culling of local post offices, and if the Royal Mail experiences a lengthy strike, or makes swingeing changes to its price structures, the victims could be the subscription magazines.

Mr Murdoch has recently entered the subscription fray in rather a grand way. His most recent acquisition is the *Wall Street Journal*, the mighty and influential financial newspaper, which he wants to take international. The subscription offer, run in *The Times*, makes an impressive pitch: 'The US edition of the *Wall Street Journal* is now on sale in Central London, which means you can read it before your colleagues and competitors in New York even wake up.' The headline is 'They snooze. They lose'. A six-month subscription comes at the 'special' price of £270. However, the paper can only be ordered in London postcodes EC, WC, W1, W2 and E14. Tycoons who live in Esher need not apply.

The *Financial Times* developed a similar scheme over ten years ago. It offers readers delivery of the *FT* by 7 a.m. within the M25 and in the Home Counties. There is a delivery charge, but that can be offset by cover price discounts and deals on FT.com subscriptions. The *Financial Times* has a minority stake in the distributor 2 The Door, which is the same service Murdoch uses for his new *Wall Street Journal* delivery system. The *Independent* also delivers, again through 2 The Door, a Monday to Friday service at the cost of £6, with an additional charge if you want the Saturday edition.

Murdoch is not a man to lose the advantage, and he announced in July 2008 a free delivery service by 7 a.m. every morning for *The Times* and the *Sunday Times*. The only stipulations were the M25 limit and payment by direct debit only. All copies were to be delivered in plastic bags to protect against rain and dog's piddle.

More of a sop to the news trade was Murdoch's next subscription manoeuvre in the summer of 2008. He announced a grand scheme to save 20 per cent of your newspaper bill, that is £70 a year, if you buy a subscription to *The Times* and the *Sunday Times*. You pay by direct debit or one-off transaction, and you take vouchers to your newsagent, who redeems them with News International.

These developments are changing the face of morning newspaper delivery. They are raining further blows upon newsagents, many of whom have lost their vital post office footfalls. Newsboy deliverers are increasingly difficult to recruit, but the morning delivery is essential to newspaper economics: regular buyers are gold dust, becoming addicts to a title and finding it hard to give up.

Casual buyers at the station kiosk can pick and choose and switch titles at a whim.

Newsagents have always been the backbone of magazine and newspaper sales. The cheap magazine subscription, the huge proliferation of supermarket news runs, the government's antipathy to local post offices and the new national delivery schemes are all undermining their viability, with unpredictable consequences for the magazines as well as Mr Patel.

internet and the myriad commercial television channels, they are giving the paid-for newspapers much to worry about.

Free newspapers have overcome people's innate reluctance to accept something thrust at them in the street, like the anecdote of the man on London Bridge failing to give away fivers. Back in 1968 *Queen* magazine had been purchased by the owner of a conglomerate of manufacturing companies who had the notion, strongly resisted by us directors, of giving away 5,000 copies of the magazine at Ascot racecourse on Ladies' Day as a sort of 'taster'. Only two copies were accepted, partly perhaps because women with big floppy hats were not keen to walk around encumbered by a glossy magazine.

What do you get when you have battled your way down the tube station and grabbed your morning copy of *Metro*? There will be no editorial from that morning's *Daily Mail*. *Metro* consists of sound bites, with no item filling a whole page. This is a paper for people in a hurry, probably musing about the day's work ahead and remembering to get out at the right station. An example of the speedy fare on offer is the '60 Second Interview' in which questions are shot at some celebrity – hardly an in-depth feature. There are reviews of comedy shows, the latest DVDs and last night's TV. There is no comment on any topic, no editorial leader and no columnists. You find your news scattered in snippets through the advertisement-strewn pages. If you are accustomed to reading a proper newspaper this is unsatisfying stuff, although most of the top stories of the day are there in brief. You get the television listings for that evening and all the local cinemas across the suburbs and the West End. The publication tells you what reader offers are available in today's *Daily Mail* and *Evening Standard* and carries an advertisement for *Lite*, which is the give-away version of the *Evening Standard*. You can't ask for your money back if you find it dull and unsatisfying, but it is worth every penny you didn't pay for it.

The down side of this sort of publishing is that readers may grow accustomed to this sort of freebie and may never want to buy one of the traditional morning newspapers again. The *Metro* is a successful operation for Associated Newspapers, but will they live to regret that they are building a significant population of readers who will never crave more in-depth products?

Presumably spurred on by the success of their morning give-away, Associated Newspapers risked lunchtime confusion when their *Evening Standard* street-corner vendors began offering passers-by a free paper called *Lite* even before the first editions of the *Standard* hit the streets. All was explained when Murdoch's News International launched their own free evening offering, the *London Paper*. So now, as you enter an Underground station or a mainline terminus, two newspapers are thrust upon you. If you take one you feel obliged to take the other from the next distributor holding a pile of papers under his or her arm. You don't really discover what you have got until you get on your train, having walked past the old news vendor still endeavouring to purvey the paid-for *Evening Standard*.

As a newspaper junkie all my life I find the current appetite for free-sheets rather bizarre, especially since for only 50p Londoners can buy the excellent *Standard*, a paper superior to all the morning tabloids and steeped in the news and politics of London. Are people too mean to cough up 50p, or – more likely – have they lost the habit of reading serious journalism?

Lite, or *London Lite*, to dignify it with its proper title, contains little of the editorial which you will find in the traditional paper. A few major London stories may appear, but the free-sheet is more involved with the cult of celebrity and eschews the *Standard*'s coverage of city news. Instead it offers a fourteen-page entertainment section covering music, clubs, comedy and theatre. The television critic is common to both papers, and the evening's television listings are comprehensive.

Sport gets a few pages at the back, and the whole offering is superior to the Murdoch paper.

The *London Paper* is redolent of its parent paper, the *Sun*, with a very busy lifestyle and an emphasis, of course, on celebrities, in case you don't get enough of them elsewhere. It does cover politics occasionally, if very lightly. After the Labour candidate lost his deposit, coming fifth behind the British National Party, at a by-election in Henley following Boris Johnson's election as London Mayor in June 2008, the *London Paper*'s front page heading was an elegant 'Gord gets a kick in the ballots'. The mood and style of the paper are tailored to the younger commuter, offering fairly comprehensive listings of London clubs, music venues and cinemas but no theatres. There are gay columns and amateur columnists, and the paper uses texts from readers on suggested topics. It manages to present an image of busyness and buzz, and it is not difficult to assimilate the lot almost between stations. But you cannot complain: it's all free, folks.

I spent a little time last summer watching the big hand-outs at some of the busiest give-away points. A news vendor at London Bridge station was selling the *Evening Standard* right opposite the give-aways. When I asked her how she felt about the competition she shrugged and laughed, saying that *Lite* and her paper came from the same company. Pressed a little, she said the situation was ridiculous and admitted that she had suffered badly from falling sales. I had a very similar reaction from most of the newsagents I asked, many giving me their reply in indignant tones.

A more low-profile success has been the free distribution of *City AM*. As the name implies, this is a newspaper in the square mile and immediate environs, sometimes handed out and sometimes left in stands. The editorial appeal is purely financial, and it waves two fingers at the majesty of the *Financial Times*. Over 100,000 copies are given out every weekday, and the publishers aim to reach a circulation of over 150,000 by moving into the affluent venture capital belt of Mayfair and Belgravia. Flushed with their success, the private investors behind the paper are considering taking on a second city when the financial climate improves. Revenues are up, and the paper is now in profit. The management announced in the summer of 2008 that they were reducing the number of hand-out distributors from about 200 to 115. Maybe they foresaw that in future their workforce might be drawn from the ranks of displaced city bankers.

Another free niche paper appeared on the streets of London in 2007. *Sport* was handed out on Fridays to anyone interested. It is a good-quality magazine but has an uphill task in competing with the time advantage enjoyed by the daily papers (free or paid-for).

Another free weekly is *ShortList*, a lifestyle magazine aimed at men. It was founded by Mike Soutar, an escapee from IPC, and is distributed in eleven cities, including Manchester, Edinburgh and Glasgow, as well as London. The circulation has been estimated at half a million. Some of these circulation estimates for free magazines can be a little hazy, but the Audit Bureau of Circulation has now introduced a rule preventing free titles claiming for copies that were returned without being handed out. This would seem an obvious ruling – advertisers can hardly be happy to think of copies never leaving the hands of the street distributors.

On the face of it, the free newspapers phenomenon is insane. About 1 million copies flood the streets of London each night, turning the economics of newspaper publishing on its head, not to mention causing a massive litter problem for the Underground and rail network. Do they have a long-term future? A rumour that the *London Paper* may close was recently denied by James Murdoch, the new boss at News International. 'There are no plans. There is nothing like that on the agenda,' he said, pointing to the popularity of the paper among its readership in London. The situation is reminiscent of the Maxwell–Rothermere battle of the London evenings when Maxwell blinked first and retired from the fray.

But perhaps the frees are the wave of the future, and all national newspapers will head the same way. The *Evening Standard* itself could go free: it was giving away over 100,000 copies on average ('bulk sales') to bolster its ABC figure to 300,000 in the middle of 2008. It also introduced the 'Eros Reward Card': by signing up to a monthly direct debit, readers could pay 15p for their evening paper against the usual price of 50p. You only have to flash your card at sellers around central London, the City and Canary Wharf displaying the Eros sign. They claimed 2,600 outlets were participating in the scheme.

Which newspaper tycoon will set the cat among the pigeons with a completely free quality morning paper?

9

THE STATE OF THE ART

THE ELEVEN NATIONAL DAILY NEWSPAPERS AND
ELEVEN SUNDAYS STILL SELL 80 MILLION COPIES
EACH WEEK BETWEEN THEM
–
THE QUALITY SUNDAYS PUT ON WEIGHT

A cold shudder must have run through newspaper offices in the early summer of 2008. This was nothing to do with circulation, nothing to do with a shortage of advertising, nothing to do with Google, social networking and the internet in general. The shudder was caused by an arch-rival in the media world. The BBC announced the end of *What the Papers Say*, the second longest-running programme on British television. It was not the closure itself that hurt; it was how the Beeb explained its decision. 'The show is not relevant in the digital age. It has had a great run with us, but the environment has changed dramatically and so has the way our audience consumes the news.'

This was a slap in the face for an industry that has undergone huge changes in production techniques over the past few years, and still sells about 80 million newspapers every week. There are eleven national dailies and eleven national, catering for extremely diverse audiences. Are they still fit and well? Let us take a wander through the facts and figures and look at their profiles, warts and all.

- *Sun* This is Mr Murdoch's baby. It boasts a circulation of 3.1 million, with an adult readership of 8 million. The median age of its readers is 43, with a male/female ratio of 56/44. The Editor is female, still a rarity in today's Fleet Street. It enjoys a lot of free publicity because thousands of parked lorries always seem to have a copy of the paper lying on the dashboard. Page 3 still has a display of breasts, but the celeb factor is restrained to a couple of pages. Deidre is the problem lady (pondering issues such as 'Sex on the kitchen floor with my mother-in-law'), but what do you want for 30p? This is Britain's biggest-selling daily – which says much about the state of the nation.

- *Daily Mail* The Rothermere paper sells 2.3 million copies and is read by 5.5 million people with a median age of 54. When you pick the paper up, you almost feel it bristling with indignation at the outrageous doings of local officials, the government and petty bureaucracy in general. The letters from readers back up this indignation and the general sense that things aren't what they used to be. The paper carries theme issues: Monday – Lifestyle, Tuesday – Good Health, Wednesday – Money and so on. Its indignation has lasted since 1896, so it may be with us for many years yet. The Saturday issue is weighed down with holiday ads.

- *Daily Mirror* This is our third-largest selling paper. It makes a great deal of news itself with its constant internal financial problems. Maybe the ghost of Robert Maxwell haunts the building, soaking wet as he tramps the corridors. The paper enjoyed an editorial make-over in 2008, which smartened it up. The median reader's age is 49. It was launched by Northcliffe back in 1903 as a women's paper, but the male/female ratio is now 54/46. The strapline is 'A Better Read

Guaranteed', which can't be legally binding. There are no tits, which is probably why it undersells the *Sun*. It is very keen on celebs.

- *Daily Telegraph* Surprisingly, at 860,000 it has the next largest daily net sale. Owned by the mysterious Barclay Twins, the *Telegraph* is middle class and British to the core. The median reader's age is 57, with a male/female ratio of 56/44. The readership is 2.1 million. It is very keen on sport and business. An important feature is the Deaths page: this paper buries significantly more bodies than *The Times*. *Telegraph* readers are steadfast and loyal to the paper, quite unshakeable in their conviction that Mr Murdoch's paper is inferior to theirs. It insists on staying broadsheet, which may be just bloody-mindedness.

- *Daily Express* This is the ghost of Lord Beaverbrook's beloved Empire-fixated daily, now owned by Mr Richard Desmond. It sells 740,000 copies, which gives it the fourth-largest daily sale, way behind the *Daily Mail* which it would passionately like to overtake. The median reader's age is 56 and the sex ratio 51/49. The core readership is younger than the *Mail*. It sells at a much-trumpeted 40 pence, 'ten pence cheaper than the *Daily Mail* and ten times better'. Basically it copies its rival's make-up and style, with a Hickey column identical in style to the *Mail*'s Ephraim Hardcastle's column. It also misuses an old *Express* name in its painfully unfunny Beachcomber column, a travesty of the old master. The Letters to the Editor are not as 'flog them' as the *Mail*, but the politics are still right wing. Interestingly, the famous Crusader is still on the front page and the royal coat of arms is used over the leader column.

- *The Times* This is the old lady of the dailies, launched in 1785. Like many a dowager, in June 2008 it felt the need of a make-over, a bit of plastic surgery and a nice facelift – nothing vulgar, mind you, just a general smartening and modernizing. There were some complaints about moving the leader columns to page 2. Personally I thought this was sensible – I would even have voted for page 3, as right-hand pages are more prominent. There is an excellent Daily Universal Register page with a lovely hodgepodge of information. Times 2 is now a daily magazine covering lifestyle and the arts. The letters page, both barmy and authoritative, is as readable as ever, and the crossword remains the best in the world. The circulation is just over 600,000, and the median reader's age is 48. The sex ratio is 58/42, and the North/ South split 40/60. Readership is 1.6 million, and at 70p the paging is generous. On Saturday they go to town with a colour magazine, the *Knowledge* magazine, featuring the arts and several leisure sections, including a book section.
- *Daily Star* Richard Desmond found this in his stocking when he took over the two *Express* newspapers. It sells 726,000 copies to a median-age readership of 39, the lowest of all the nationals. The male/female readership ratio is an unsurprising 70/30. This is downmarket stuff, with plenty of bums and tits, lots of celeb chat and sport – not the paper Lord Matthews intended when he launched it back in 1978.
- *Financial Times* The pink'un delivers exactly as expected for a modern City newspaper. The median age of its readers is a low 44, and the core readership is business decision-makers, over-25 and ABC1. The sex ratio is 74/26, so it still caters, metaphorically, for bowler hats and rolled umbrellas.

makes the claim on the front page 'One big newspaper, one big magazine'. This basically means that it is a one-section newspaper, a dig at the broadsheets with all their bits and pieces. Sales are a low 200,000, with a readership of 760,000. The median reader's age is 40 and the male/female split is 61/39 with a 60 per cent sale in the South. The magazine section, called 'The New Review', carries all the usual Sunday newspaper baggage. As with its daily sister, the overall effect is a little grey.

- *Mail on Sunday* This is the Rothermere Sunday. It had a weak start back in 1982 but has grown up to be the surprise success of the category, with the second highest circulation at 2,206,000. It enjoys an adult readership of nearly 6 million with a median age of 50. The core readership is BC1C2 and the sex ratio is exactly 50/50; 70 per cent of readers live in the South. You get a meaty package for your highly priced £1.50: a chunky main paper, a Part Two which carries reviews and puzzles, separate 'Home' and 'Property' sections and a glossy entertainment guide called 'Live'. A star attraction is 'You', a glossy magazine section entirely aimed at women. This is well researched and presented and generally entertaining.

- *Sunday Express* Launched by Lord Beaverbrook in 1918, the paper is now in the hands of Richard Desmond. It sells 655,000 copies with an adult readership of 1.8 million. The median age is 54 and the sex split, like the *Mail on Sunday*, is exactly 50/50. Tactically it has its eyes on the Rothermere market, and the front page claims that it is 20p cheaper than its rival. Politics are comfortably right wing and the editorial formula is familiar, with sections on finance, reviews, etc. The colour magazine is formula stuff, bulked out with the ubiquitous telly listings. This once great newspaper is now very ordinary and routine.

- *People* The surprise is that 658,000 shell out 90p each Sunday for this contribution to the media. Launched in 1881, it has a core readership of C1C2D adults with a median age of 52. The wafer-thin colour magazine section called 'Take It Easy' is pathetic, mostly TV listings. The main paper carries little display advertising and the production is poor. This is the walking wounded of the Sundays.

- *Sunday Mirror* When my mother was a girl this was called the *Sunday Pictorial* and was launched by Northcliffe back in 1903. It sells a surprising 1.3 million copies with a readership of over 4 million. The core readership is identical in class to the *People*. Celebrity is the name of the game here, with the news pages sprinkled with all the usual suspects. The paper also carries a colour magazine section entitled 'Celebs on Sunday'. Sport is fairly prominent, which explains their sex split of 57/43. All the usual puzzles and all the customary Sunday features are present.

- *Daily Star on Sunday* This is another contribution from Richard Desmond. There are lots of bottoms, bosoms (but no bare tits) and sport and lashings of sexy celeb gossip. It also carries a flimsy magazine section called 'Take Five', which has very sketchy TV programme listings. The paper, like the daily, proclaims itself as the official Big Brother organ, which gives it some randy inside news. Circulation is 389,000 and the median reader's age is 36. The geographical ratio is reversed from the other Sundays: 53% in the North.

- *Sunday Sport* Well, what would you expect? For 80p you get a trace of news, acres of naked tits and bottoms and some sport. The advertising is sexually adventurous, which probably excludes it from being on sale at your more respectable newsagent. The day of rest is now the day of the breast.

- *News of the World* Mr Murdoch's other Sunday newspaper, once upon a time selling a cracking 8 million copies, now still nets 3.1 million. Ironically, the readership *is* 8 million. The median age is 43 and the sex ratio 52/48. This is a paper that likes to sensationalize and scoop the competition. Because of the circulation and readership data, it carries a good share of advertising, compared to most of the down-market tabloids. There is plenty of gossip and, of course, celebrities. It is big on sport, but overall it is a respectable if saucy newspaper and its arch reputation must help sales along. A cheeky addition is a little colour magazine section called, inventively, the 'News of the World Magazine', which it proclaims is Britain's biggest weekly glossy, a claim it fails to substantiate in format or paging.

Of course, a book cannot long remain up to date with circulation figures. I have based these figures on the latest Audit Bureau of Circulation and National Readership Survey data available at the time of writing. Some of them may be risibly optimistic by the time you read this.

It is quite an enlightening experience to spend time exploring the twenty-two specimens that make up the national press. Two basic impressions remain in the slightly numbed mind of the researcher: the editorial standard of the so-called red-tops is often depressingly low, saturated as they are with celebrity nonsense, but the 'qualities' score high points with their wide variety of erudite and readable columnists.

But all newspaper circulations are heading downwards. (The only exception at the time of writing was the 'soaraway' *Sun*, which showed a mid-year spurt, influenced by price cutting and heavy promotion.) All the rest of the dailies showed losses year on year ranging from a tiny 0.1 per cent to a socking 6.7 per cent. The Sundays' losses have been getting even heavier, especially a depressing 14.8 per cent decline for the *Independent on Sunday*. Across-the-board declines in sales cannot be put down to editorial blips, so the trend is naturally a worry for the Fleet Street tycoons.

One characteristic does stand out when you read the Sundays *en masse*. They all follow the same trail – the same sections appearing in all the qualities with sedate inevitability. New ground is seldom broken in presentation or ideas. The red-top Sundays are just depressing. As news seldom seems to break at weekends, the tabloids are low-standard magazines with lots of sports pages. And every Sunday has to have a colour magazine, presumably as a prestige circulation item. They range from flimsy TV listings to full-blown magazines, but the latter lack the original punch which used to make the early *Sunday Times* colour magazine so unmissable.

The standard of the Saturday editions of the dailies is generally higher than their sister Sundays. Saturday used to be a circulation black hole, but now it has become a hot date for readers, particularly of the quality press. Is this the future: Saturdays the favourite purchase, Sunday a bit of a yawn?

10

ARE MAGAZINES GETTING BORING?

THERE ARE PLENTY OF MAGAZINES BUT
NOT MUCH VARIETY

–

FOR MANY TITLES CIRCULATION IS ON THE SLIDE

–

THE WOMEN'S PRESS LACKS ORIGINALITY;
CELEBRITY GOSSIP IS NOT ENOUGH

–

INNOVATION IS NEEDED ACROSS THE INDUSTRY

I once said the consumer magazine market was characterized by 'bulging bookstalls'. This is still true, but what are the shelves bulging with today? When I made my remark, the profusion of magazines was a result of innovation and trail-blazing initiatives, reaching virgin audiences with exciting editorial concepts.

Today a glance at the display of titles on show exposes more old hat than you'd find in a Paris milliner's window. The groups of titles are depressingly familiar: the tiresome 'celebrity' mags, still flogging their gossip about supposedly interesting people; the women's weeklies, sliding into the celebrity mire; the men's monthlies and weeklies, with a few exceptions still mammary-obsessed; the domestic monthlies with their seasonal editorial mix; the young women's monthlies preoccupied as ever with sex; the television listings; those bizarre 'real-life' magazines; and the tiny but brave purveyors of serious journalism.

The magazine business appears to lack the editorial inventiveness to develop new products and send many of the older ones into graceful retirement. The fact that some of the tottering titles of yesteryear are still producing profit here and there is not reason enough to expend editorial and business energy on them that would be better used launching new magazines.

The 'credit crunch' has taken its toll of advertising across all the media, but in addition the six-monthly ABC figures are warning that the magazine readership is becoming dissatisfied with the merchandise on offer. Even the celebrity magazines are beginning to lose their shine: the seven major titles in this genre dropped nearly 700,000 sales between them according to the mid-year figures for 2008, with only *Hello!* putting on copies. And this was at a time of profligate spending on wedding coverage. 'Real-life' magazines are also experiencing a dip in popularity – maybe all those people in incestuous love affairs are beginning to lose their appeal. Overall the top fifty paid-for consumer magazines lost 3.4 per cent of their circulation, with only eleven titles gaining sales, despite all that subscription activity.

So what can a publisher do when a once-successful magazine starts to bleed readers? Current thinking seems to be: 'Give it a new look!' That old warhorse *Prima* lost 6 per cent of its sales, so National Magazines went for a new look and added thirty pages. BBC's *Focus* also announced a new look, as did *Reader's Digest*, whose once proud 1.7 million circulation is down to 640,000, of which 580,000 are subscriptions. The new Editor announced that there would be 'an increased use of content created in-house as opposed to using content sourced from third party publications'. That was, of course, the traditional worldwide policy of the magazine, hence its title.

As if to illustrate the widening gap between rich and poor, the upmarket fashion and social glossies continue to succeed. The four titles, *Vogue, Harper's Bazaar, Elle* and *Vanity Fair*, are all prospering, with a bulge in advertising paging and increasing or steady circulation performance. They are still benefiting from the boom in the fortunes of the mega-rich, and advertising budgets have soared to meet the demand. Tiffany increased its UK advertising spend by £200,000 to £1.9 million, Louis Vuitton luggage is currently spending £1.7 million and Jimmy Choo upped its advertising budget by £50,000. The top cosmetic advertisers announced record new budgets (Clinique up to £2.1 million), and the top hotels are not far behind with the Ritz Carlton nearly doubling its spend. The magazine glossies take more than their fair share of all this new money. The four titles are selling 634,000 copies between them, so this is one fortunate category of magazine publishing that has no need to change its editorial formula.

The other side of the coin is the men's magazines, which enjoyed an unexpected surge in the 1990s, with new titles and burgeoning sales. *GQ* from Condé Nast sits at the top of the market, maintaining a circulation of 130,000, with the other American import *Esquire* way behind at 58,000. These titles are literate and upmarket. The two men's fitness titles sell 300,000 copies between them, heavily weighted towards *Men's Health*. The losers are the lads' magazines, all dropping chunks of circulation. *Loaded*, the IPC title that began sensationally in 1994, full of coarse language and sexual pizzazz appealing to the New Bloke, recently dropped 20 per cent of sales year on year, down to a humiliating 95,000. The Dennis contribution to male culture, *Maxim*, dropped over 50 per cent of news-stand sales and could claim only 43,500 copies on the ABC. But what of the weeklies, those brave launches into a hitherto untapped market? They both shed sales, *Zoo* by 14 per cent, but together they manage to appeal to just over 400,000 buyers lured in by the nakedness on their covers. It cannot be a coincidence that these falling circulations have been counter-balanced by the success of the two give-away titles *ShortList* and *Sport*.

The television listings magazines, in the face of intense competition for programme information from the daily press and the electronic programme guides, still keep their heads above water, with the *Radio Times, TV Choice* and *What's on TV* shifting a combined 3.7 million copies weekly. The other seven titles in the group do not count for much in the scheme of things.

Women, on the whole, stay loyal to their magazines. The only major loss in sales has come from Bauer's *More*, which by 2008 had sensationally dropped over 37 per cent from year to year, having moved from fortnightly to weekly and shifted overtly into the celebrity market. To be fair, the magazine is still selling 60 per cent more copies as a weekly than it previously did as a fortnightly. National Magazines ran into trouble with their 'real-life' *Reveal*, which shed 21 per cent of its circulation, so they relaunched it as 'the celebrity magazine written by celebrities'.

With some exceptions, the homes and gardening market remains strong, with the BBC *Gardeners' World* leaping ahead by 27 per cent. *Country Living*, the magazine I launched in 1978, has reached 200,000 sales, partly through lively subscription selling and a successful extension into country shows.

The news and current affairs magazines have been having a patchy time. The *Spectator* has reached a circulation high of 77,000, but as only 11,000 are sold on the news-stands one can assume heavy subscription promotion. The same consideration applies to *The Week*, now selling 150,000 copies but only 11,000 on the news-stands. A disappointment was a decline in *Big Issue* sales, which dropped by

23 per cent. The *Economist* and *Time* both lost news-stand sales but maintained healthy overall sales.

Publishers trumpet their bi-annual ABC figures if they are attractively up and talk fast if they are not. As Steve Barrett, the Editor of *Media Week*, wrote when commenting on the six-monthly figures in August 2008:

> Magazines are no longer just print products – they are brands spanning multiple platforms, including the web, mobile, radio and even TV, but, as with newspapers, measurement systems haven't caught up. *Maxim*, for example, posted a staggering circulation decline of almost 60% but Dennis Publishing chief executive James Tye counters that the magazine reaches one million people across all platforms . . . only about 5% of magazines currently commission an ABCe audit. Until all publishers buy into the ABCe system and get regular audits, they can hardly complain that print ABCs aren't representing their brand reach properly.

Indeed, the very word 'platform' meant nothing, except to a railway enthusiast, until the first adventurous publishers purchased a website and recorded their 'hits'. Figures for internet activity seem to differ widely. *Auto Trader* records some 10 million hits a month, while *FHM* has reported 2 million, *Heat* 1.5 and *Zoo* and *Nuts* 1 million or so each. Canny publishers can cover their tracks when explaining a drop in circulation by producing ABCe figures to substantiate the importance of their 'brand'. Of course, if a magazine collapses, so do the brand extensions. The only real test of the success or failure or a magazine is the copy sale, whether by subscription or at news-stands.

With 'platforms' or not, magazine publishers still have an uphill struggle to keep their titles solvent. Quite a lot of price cutting, either overt or covert, has been going on, and subscriptions, as we have seen, are now paramount for many titles. The news trade is still important to the publisher, even if their relationship is not as cosy as once it was owing to the conspicuous flogging of subscriptions in the magazines themselves, including within the copies on the newsagent's counter.

The supermarkets also loom large in the magazine mix. There was a scare in the summer of 2008 when Asda informed magazine publishers of plans to request two pages of editorial or advertising each month in the titles of its choosing, and in addition it proposed that shop space given over to a distributor's titles would be subject to a 'space contribution' of £10,000 paid to the supermarket. Furthermore, Asda was proposing levying a space contribution for each new Asda store opening of £2,500 per title. Publishers were bursting blood vessels when these suggestions were reported, and the story was quickly disowned by the company. But publishers beware! Asda alone control 4.8 per cent of the UK sale of magazines. Once the supermarkets sniff blood, outrageous demands might be laid at the door of the publishing industry, and the supermarkets are growing dangerously dominant in the sale of newspapers and magazines.

Of course, publishers can still rely on retail newsagents, which still sell about 30 per cent of consumer magazines, and on the multiples W.H. Smith *et al*. The supermarkets were late in the magazine selling game but have made up for their tardiness by embracing the medium as an important part of their product range. Perhaps obsolescent magazines such as *Woman* and *Woman's Own*, and the celebrity weeklies, would not be with us today except for the convenience with which they can be added to the supermarket trolley.

Although it slightly pains me to write it, the trade owe a big debt to Richard Desmond and his Northern and Shell company. *OK!*, *Star* and *New!* pump out weekly sales of a combined 1.2 million copies. *OK!* has twenty overseas editions, with a promised twenty-eight to

The MailOnline claims 5.09 million unique users a month in the UK; that is roughly the same number as buy a copy of the *Mail* (circulation 2.23 million) over just two days. 'One industry estimate reckons a newspaper reader added is worth £80.00 and a net user added only £2.00. Even heavyweights like the *New York Times* can't push internet revenues over 10% of the whole. And meanwhile, if you were a high street big name in trouble, where would you put the weight of ad spend as you struggle to get things moving again? Don't sell ITV short just yet, I think.'

None the less big doubts hang over the future for all the media. There is particular gloom about the regional press, which is vulnerable to a sharp fall in classified revenue as a result of the recession in the jobs and housing market but more sinisterly by the encroachment of the internet with its effective response rates. Some of the more sombre prophecies foretell the closure of titles and entire publishing companies in 2009.

In all the years I worked in magazines and newspapers there was always a rosy-spectacled, if cautious, optimism that good times were just around the corner and that advertisers would always want to buy space if you had the right product. But maybe, as Noël Coward used to sing sardonically, 'Bad times are just around the corner,' and many of the missing advertisers may not return to the print press.

The newspaper industry received another piece of bad news in the summer of 2008 with the sudden death of the weekly trade paper for journalists, the *Press Gazette*. The cause of its demise was purely financial; there had been a couple of changes of ownership, including the partnership of Matthew Freud and Piers Morgan who were reported to have lost £1 million during their short period as proprietors. But one senior newspaper executive told the *Guardian*: 'There is a whiff of death about an industry that can't even sustain its own trade magazine.'

Who can say that the world owes the print media a living? By the time the current recession has finally passed, many magazines could have folded and, heaven forbid, one or two daily or Sunday newspapers may have given up the ghost. Things already look pretty bad. The Barclay twins bought the *Telegraph* group for £655 million in 2004, but in four years its worth had dropped to £100 million. The solid old *Daily Mirror* regularly makes the financial headlines with collapsing shares and a drooping circulation. Murdoch and Rothermere are giving away over a million copies of their papers every weekday evening. There is talk of doing away with sub-editors as journalists transmit their own material ready for publication, and the merger of print and internet journalism is already under way.

As advertisers grow more coy about lashing out their hard-earned budgets, some of the quality papers may face a stark choice: put up the cover price to maintain the product or cut the size of the paper. The publishers will probably feel that £1 would not be unreasonable for *The Times* or the *Telegraph*, and are the *Mail* and the *Evening Standard* at 50p really worth 50p less than the *Independent* or 40p less than the *Guardian*?

The media have themselves to blame when it comes to perceived value. If you give away newspapers, however crass, or constantly run magazine subscription offers cutting the cover prices by chunks, the reading public will accept your gifts but think a little less of the product. Certainly some newspapers seem unnecessarily bulky and burdened with too many supplements, particularly at weekends.

The recent high sales of Saturday editions have led Peter Preston, writing in the *British Journalism Review*, to make the provocative suggestion that some newspaper groups could stop publishing daily editions and put out weekend papers instead on a Saturday or a Sunday. Maybe the traditional Sunday is doomed!

The next couple of years will surely see a new dawn – rosy or otherwise. To sell newspapers and magazines you need outlets, and, as we have seen, the traditional ways of flogging newsprint and coated paper are already severely challenged. Twenty years ago there were 21,000 post offices in the UK; now there are just 11,500. Traditionally sub-post offices were run by small business people who efficiently sold magazines and delivered our newspapers to the front door. But today many newsagents have morphed into convenience stores open all hours, content to sell newspapers and magazines as a sideshow to the profitable baked beans and fresh milk but not committed to making newspaper deliveries.

Asda sells over 1 million magazines every week, and the mighty Tesco has a 13 per cent market share. The supermarkets now have huge buying power, and publishers are nervous about their commercial relationships with them in the future. Their passion for selling subscriptions, almost at any price, is a response to this potential threat.

Of course, no amount of ingenuity in developing new ways of moving their stock will suffice unless the publishers have high-quality products to sell. As we have seen, many of the popular Sundays, in particular, are wanting in originality. Many newspapers and magazines have simply copied each other's ideas and presentation. Some are rather tired, and their commercial usefulness is doubtful. To quote Noël Coward again: 'Why *must* the show go on? You've bored us all for years . . .'

Let us hope that if there is to be some weeding out of the old and infirm, it will make room for the new, the fresh and the original. From leafy Kensington to the commercial buzz of Canary Wharf, we await the Next Big Thing.

POSTSCRIPT

SOME MILLENNIUM THOUGHTS

Back in 1999, on the eve of the millennium, I was approached by a Canadian broadcasting company which was planning an international programme to review the world's most influential magazines. I was asked to name six or seven British magazines which I felt had made a positive contribution to the world of magazines. The titles could be extant or extinct. This was my choice. I am sure many readers of this book will fervently disagree!

- *The Englishwoman's Domestic Magazine*, 1852. This was the magazine launched by Samuel Beeton, husband of Mrs Beeton. His launch changed the face of women's magazines of the period, which had been directed at the very fashionable lady with an interest in society and the arts. The *EDM* cost an attractive twopence against the more customary shilling and opened up an untapped readership with a magazine aimed at the ordinary housewife. Within three years it was selling 50,000, copies and it can be claimed to have invented the popular women's magazine.
- *Punch*, 1841. You can't leave *Punch* off the list. What a survivor through the years, from those tortuous Victorian puns and jokes through the world wars with astringent political cartoons. This was a humorous magazine managed over

the years by a series of famous editors. A look back at those dusty bound volumes impresses with its biting humour and social awareness.

- *Economist*, 1843. My last Victorian choice; an august journal which has always set a benchmark in the financial world and which since the Second World War has considerably extended its global influence. It has seen off many a competitor over the years. It represents the gold standard in serious magazine publishing.

- *Country Life*, 1906. So British you almost have to stand up when it comes into the room! This is the glossy's glossy, representing a golden lifestyle of magnificent country houses and agricultural prosperity. It has always presented an all-round picture of upper-class life for the countryman: racing, farming, husbandry, the arts, gardening, motoring and so on. Most importantly, it is still with us today. Even those of us who can only peek at the lifestyle through the window must be impressed by its grandeur.

- *Picture Post*, 1938. This classic magazine made a tremendous impact during its short life, a mere nineteen years. It brought a polished realism to photo-journalism and made its considerable reputation during the war years on the home and the battle fronts. The magazine produced many of our great photographers. In the post-war period it reflected the grim social conditions in many parts of the country. Its closure left a gap that has never been filled.

- *Private Eye*, 1961. Surely the *Punch de nos jours*! Along with the BBC programme *That Was the Week That Was* it spearheaded the satire boom of the 1960s. Vulgar, schoolboyish, scatological, impish, iconoclastic – there *has* to be such a magazine, and *Private Eye* stands alone.

We sometimes deride it, but how we need it! It must never close.

- *Radio Times*, 1923. A British classic for eighty-five years which has stood the test of time and weathered broadcasting upheavals. Now surrounded by competing magazines. Reliable, readable and authoritative. As British as the BBC itself.

AFTERWORD

I wrote in my preface that no book about the print media could ever be up to date. How right I was! In the four months since I finished the book the financial situation has been severely hard on the press.

In January Deloittes published their gloomy forecast that 'one in ten print publications will be forced to slash publication, move online or close entirely'. GroupM, a media and marketing forecaster, opined that local newspapers will see a 20 per cent fall in advertising revenues.

The end-of-the-year ABC figures for 2008 showed a 5 per cent year-on-year circulation slide for the national dailies and 6 per cent for the Sundays. (The *Sunday Times* was the exception.) Trinity Mirror announced the closure of twenty-eight of its regional newspapers, and in a unique situation the *Independent* and the *Independent on Sunday* moved into the *Daily Mail* offices in Kensington to save costs, sharing back-office services, although there was no suggestion of an editorial link-up.

All the nationals were reporting or threatening lay-offs, redundancies and pay freezes. The *Daily Sport* reported that it had broken one of its banking covenants and the circulation had dropped to 80,000.

The January editions of the newspapers, and the January and February issues of most of the consumer magazines, showed a bleak downturn in their advertising. Magazines estimate suggest a loss of

20–30 per cent loss of revenue for the year ahead. The regional press reported sliding losses of classified advertising, partly owing to the general economic situation but with many categories moving to the internet. Newspaper cover prices are on the move with *The Times* increasing to 90 pence and the *Independent* to £1.

The first big newspaper story of 2009 was the sale of the London *Evening Standard* by the Daily Mail group to the Russian billionaire Alexander Lebedev, ex-KGB and part owner of the Russian newspaper *Noyova Gazeta*. The deal with Rothermere gives him a 75.1 per cent interest in the London paper, which he bought for a nominal £1. The *Mail* announced it would retain a 24.9 per cent interest in the *Standard* and 'provide commercial services such as printing and distribution'. (Some irony here: it was the latter service which would seem to have led to the downfall of the paper.) Mr Lebedev insisted that he would not interfere with the editorial control of the publication. The new Editor would be Geordie Greig from the *Tatler*. Many staff redundancies were forecast.

Much of the consumer magazine industry faced 2009 with a New Year circulation hangover. The ABC figures for the past year showed, in general, a dismal picture. The upmarket fashionable glossies, bolstered by vigorous price-slashing subscription selling, kept their figures constant. But the traditional women's weeklies all saw losses averaging 8 per cent year on year across the sector. The reading public's love affair with celebrity culture seems to be fading with *OK!* shedding 200,000 copies on their ABC figure year on year. Right across the women's magazines the minus signs dominate the statistics. Men's magazines, apart the fitness titles, all showed worrying and substantial losses, including those for the two new weeklies. Give-away newspapers continue to feed the commuter market with their sound-bite editorial style, their obsessions with celebrities, with health and beauty advertorials and their contribution to the recycling industry.

To date, no national newspaper has closed or merged as a result of this latest recession, although this state of affairs may have changed by the year's end. We live in interesting times!

FURTHER READING

Bower, Tom, *Maxwell: The Outsider*, Aurum Press, London, 1988

Braithwaite, Brian, Noelle Walsh and Glyn Davies (eds), *The Home Front: The Best of Good Housekeeping 1939–1945*, Ebury Press, London, 1987

Braithwaite, Brian, *Women's Magazines: The First 300 Years*, Peter Owen, London, 1995

Brendon, Piers, *The Life and Death of the Press Barons*, Secker and Warburg, London, 1982

Coleridge, Nicholas, *Paper Tigers*, William Heinemann, London, 1993

Crewe, Quentin, *The Frontiers of Privilege*, William Collins, London, 1961

Cudlipp, Hugh, *At Your Peril*, Weidenfeld and Nicolson, London, 1962

de Courcy, Anne, *Snowdon*, Weidenfeld and Nicolson, London, London, 2008

Edwards, Robert, *Goodbye, Fleet Street*, Jonathan Cape, London, 1988

Edwards, Ruth Dudley, *Newspapermen*, Secker and Warburg, London, 2003

Evans, Harold, *Good Times, Bad Times*, Weidenfeld and Nicolson, London, 1983

Evans, Harry, and Ray Boston, *The Essential Fleet Street*, Cassell, London, 1990

Glover, Stephen, *Paper Dreams*, Jonathan Cape, London, 1993

Griffiths, Dennis, *300 Years of Fleet Street 1702–2002*, London Press Club, London, 2002

Henry, Harry, *Behind the Headlines: The Business of the British Press*, Associated Business Press, London, 1978

Hopkinson, Tom, *Picture Post, 1938–1950*, Penguin Books, Harmondsworth, 1985

James, Eric, *Stop Press*, André Deutsch, London, 1980

Kee, Robert, *The Picture Post Album*, Barrie and Jenkins, London, 1989

Kelsey, Linda, *Was It Good for You, Too? Thirty Years of Cosmopolitan Women*, Robson Books, London, 2003

Hasting, Max, *Editor: An Inside Story of Newspapers*, Macmillan, London, 2002

Hamilton, Denis, *Editor in Chief*, Hamish Hamilton, London, 1989

Hopkinson, Tom, *Of This Our Time: A Journalist's Story*, Hutchinson, London, 1982

Randall, Mike, *The Funny Side of the Street*, Bloomsbury, London, 1988

Symons, Julian, *Horatio Bottomley*, Cresset Press, London, 1955

Taylor, S.J., *The Great Outsiders: Northcliffe, Rothermere and the Daily Mail*, Weidenfeld and Nicolson, London, 1996

Webb, Kaye (ed.), *Lilliput Goes to War*, Hutchinson, London, 1986

INDEX